Force M

From the film b

Adapted for the stage by Tim Price

methuen | drama

LONDON · NEW YORK · OXFORD · NEW DELHI · SYDNEY

METHUEN DRAMA
Bloomsbury Publishing Plc
50 Bedford Square, London, WC1B 3DP, UK
1385 Broadway, New York, NY 10018, USA
29 Earlsfort Terrace, Dublin 2, Ireland

BLOOMSBURY, METHUEN DRAMA and the Methuen
Drama logo are trademarks of Bloomsbury Publishing Plc

First published in Great Britain 2021

Cover design by Hugo Glendinning/AKA

A catalogue record for this book is available from the British Library.

A catalog record for this book is available from the Library of Congress.

ISBN: PB: 978-1-3503-2243-1
ePDF: 978-1-3503-2244-8
eBook: 978-1-3503-2245-5

Series: Modern Plays

Typeset by Mark Heslington Ltd, Scarborough, North Yorkshire
Printed and bound in Great Britain

To find out more about our authors and books visit
www.bloomsbury.com and sign up for our newsletters.

Force Majeure had its world premiere at London's Donmar Warehouse on 10 December 2021 with the following cast and creative team:

Writer	Tim Price
Director	Michael Longhurst
Designer	Jon Bausor
Lighting Designer	Lucy Carter
Sound Designer	Donato Wharton
Movement Director	Sasha Milavic Davies
Casting Director	Anna Cooper CDG

Cast

Nathalie Armin
Bo Bragason
Holly Cattle
Raffaello Degruttola
Florence Hunt
Henry Hunt
Siena Kelly
Rory Kinnear
Lyndsey Marshal
Kwami Odoom
Sule Rimi
Oliver Savell
Arthur Wilson

Writers' Thanks

Michael Longhurst, Nick Morrison, Henny Finch, Clare Slater, Elayce Ismail and all at the Donmar Warehouse and all cast and creatives. Ruben Östlund, Erik Hemmendorff, Kelly Fury, Cathy King and all at 42. Chloë Moss, Gary Marsh and Mark Jefferies.

Force Majeure

Characters

Ebba – 43
Tomas – 40
Vera – 11
Harry – 7
Charlotte – 41
Mats – 42
Jenny – 22
Brady – 20s American
Photographer/Man/Guest/Male Skier – Middle aged male
Female Skier
Receptionist
Cleaner

N/S Characters

Waitress
Hotel Guests
Stag Party

Notes

A / indicates when the next line should be spoken.

(. . .) a line in brackets should be unspoken but indicates the intention of the rest of the sentence.

Scene One

The Lobby

The mountain is permanently present looming from the back of the stage towards the front. All locations are created so that the mountain is both not there, and always there. Across the mountain ridge we can see Gazex tubes, which look like periscopes rising from the ground. Explosions from these tubes create the controlled avalanches. They should be dotted around the auditorium – and should make a booming sound as well as a flash when set off.

With suitcases around them, the family wearing ski-wear stand arm in arm in the lobby of the hotel, admiring the view of the mountain.

Harry Wow.

Vera Wow.

Ebba Oh My God look at it.

Vera It's huge.

Tomas Yeah. No hiding up there.

Harry And you've skied from the top there?

Tomas Yeah. A few times. With Mats.

Harry Would you do it again?

Tomas Yeah.

Ebba Would you?

Vera Are you/ gonna do it this week?

Tomas What's that supposed to mean? I'm in shape, I'm in the same shape I was in my twenties. Did a half marathon.

Ebba *is laughing, a receptionist returns.*

Receptionist Alors, qui est la personne suivante?

Ebba He's back.

Tomas I'll go.

Ebba   No I've got the booking references and passports. You stay with the kids.

Tomas   I'll stay with the kids.

Vera   Are you gonna do it this week?

Tomas   Are *you* gonna do it this week?/ That's the question.

Vera   No way, I am not going up there. I don't even know if I want to ski on that.

Tomas   You will.

Vera   Look/ at it!

Harry   I'm skiing on it. We've come all this way; I want to go from the top with Dad and Mats. I'm getting ready now.

Harry *starts looking for kit in the bags.*

Tomas   The first time I came here I was a little older than you Vera, Granddad brought me.

Vera   Did he go from the top?

Harry   Dad! Where's my goggles?

Tomas *and* **Vera** *join* **Harry** *looking for the goggles in a dumb show.*

Charlotte *is waiting for her key at reception.*

Charlotte   Have you been on the slopes today?

Ebba   No, we've just arrived.

Charlotte   Are they yours?

Ebba   Yes. How about you?

Charlotte   Skiing or kids?

Ebba   Ugh . . . Both?

Charlotte   Yes, to kids, no to skiing!

Beat.

Oh, they're not here with me! I left them at home with my husband. I'm having a holiday on my own. They seem OK at the moment, if there's any problems they can call.

Ebba   How old are they?

Charlotte   Eleven and thirteen.

Ebba   OK! You didn't want to bring them with you?

Charlotte   Oh God no. No, I want a break from them!

Ebba   Ok! (*laughing*)

Tomas   Here you go!

Tomas *hands* **Harry** *his goggles.*

Ebba   We're here because Tomas works so much. So now he has five days with us, no distractions.

Tomas *steps away from the mess* **Harry** *has created.*

Ebba   And any minute now you'll see him reach to check his phone.

Tomas *reaches for a pocket, and another and another and then turns.*

Ebba *waves his phone.* **Tomas** *is busted.*

Ebba *and* **Charlotte** *laugh.*

Charlotte   I see!

With goggles on **Harry** *goes to* **Vera** *wanting the goggles tightened.*

Vera *and* **Harry** *turn their backs to* **Tomas**.

He then secretly waves a packet of cigarettes and indicates 'outside'.

Ebba   And now his next vice . . .

Ebba *shakes her head.*

Ebba   No! Talk to the kids! (*To* **Charlotte**.) It's like having three children.

Tomas *eyerolls hard and returns to his children.*

Tomas   Tidy this mess up Harry.

Harry   You need to get kitted up where's your goggles?

Vera   When are we gonna eat?

Tomas   Once/ Mummy's checked us in.

Harry   No, come on we have to go straight on the mountain, we're wasting time can we just go straight out? Come on Dad?

Tomas   OK/ let me talk to your mother first.

Harry   Yes! Where's your/ goggles Dad?

Charlotte   Enjoy your holiday.

Charlotte *leaves.*

Ebba   You too! Have a great holiday.

Ebba *picks up her keys.*

Ebba   Got them let's go.

Tomas   Kids grab/ your cases!

Harry   I've got the boot bag/ come on let's go!

Vera   Isn't there a man to carry our cases?

Tomas   Yes Vera me.

Ebba   I told you if you let her have the big case she'll just fill it.

Harry   Come on!

Tomas   Harry it's not gonna carry itself.

Harry *runs back for his case.* **Ebba** *goes for the stairs.*

Tomas   Ebba, the lift's here.

Ebba   Can we take the stairs?

Tomas   With all this?

Ebba *is anxious, but* **Tomas** *leads* **Vera** *and* **Harry** *into the lift.*
Reluctantly **Ebba** *follows.*

Cue music – In the lift, the family pulls from their backpacks helmets
and goggles. They step into ski boots in the lift and step out holding
ski poles.

No other normal amount of apparel can project quite as much kitsch
and aggression about patterns, colours and logos.

Once everyone is in position **Tomas** *looks behind him to the rest of*
the family.

Tomas   Everyone ready? Vera? Harry? Ebba?

Nods.

Tomas   OK, stick with me.

Movement sequence as the family skis together, in the background is
the boom of controlled avalanches from the Gazex tubes, integrated
with the sound design.

Tomas *skis with nonchalant confidence, effortlessly controlling*
himself down the slope.

Tomas   That's it Harry! Great work. Keep your skis parallel
Vera! This way guys! Isn't this great huh?

Vera *whoops!*

Tomas   That's great Vera! Lean a little more forward! Great
Harry!

Ebba   Not too fast Harry!

Tomas   He's fine! This is what we came here for right?!

Ebba *and* **Tomas** *share a smile.*

The family ski and whoop! with joy until they come to a halt.

Tomas   Well done! Well done guys!/ You looked great up there . . . so great being on the mountain together. And we all stayed together.

Ebba   That was fantastic /You're properly skiing now!

Vera   That was actually/ quite cool.

Harry   Dad, did you see me?/ I beat Vera and Mum? I'm ready for poles now Dad. Let me try yours.

Harry *grabs* **Tomas'** *pole, he doesn't let it go.*

Photographer *skis into the scene.*

Vera   Oh My God/ I nearly skied into that kid who fell over.

Tomas   Hang on Harry let everyone catch their breath.

Harry   I'll go/ faster with poles.

Tomas   Just hold/ on Harry.

Harry *tries to take* **Tomas'** *poles from him.*

Photographer (*O/S*)   Hello! Bonjour Monsieur!

Tomas   Oh, uh. Bonjour! Harry stop it. Stop it.

Harry   Just a little go.

Photographer   Vous voulez une photo?

Tomas   Uh, no maybe tomorrow.

Photographer   Yes, come on where you from?

Tomas   Sweden. *Harry.*

Ebba   Sweden!

Vera   Sweden.

Photographer   Sweden wow! Very good come on. The champion! You won the race yes?

Harry   Yes!

Photographer   What's your name?

Harry   Harry.

Photographer   Yes, Harry come on, it takes two seconds.
Let me take the picture of the champion. Don't worry it's
free no problem.

Harry   Yes! Dad I want a photo.

Tomas   Uh . . .

Photographer   This way very nice. Are you a champion
skier?/ Yes you are.

Harry   Yeah I won.

Photographer   Why don't you stand next to your brother?
Harry put your arm around your sister./ Facing me this
way?/ Very nice.

Ebba   Put your arm around Vera!

Photographer   Very nice! Big smile! 123. Very nice. Mrs,
why don't you come stand next to your daughter? And sir
next to your wife.

Tomas   No you don't/ want me.

Photographer   Yes come on, I'll make beautiful photo of
your family and the mountain. Ok, here we go 123, very
nice! Ok now, just Mr and Mrs. This way, Mr stand closer to
your wife and Mrs do you want to stand up straight? And
maybe put your arms together. Like this. That's nice! Big
smile.

Gazex tubes Boom!

Ebba   What *is* that?

Photographer   Controlled avalanches. They do them every
day. Many times.

Photographer   Big smile. 123 very nice! Ok, one more
whole family like a big choo choo train. With Harry at the
front because he is the champion skier! Big smile 123.

Photographer *moves.*

And one more this way. Look at me, big smiles. Mr, why don't you put your head on your wife like this?

Tomas *leans to* **Ebba** *and they bang heads.*

Ebba   Ow!

Photo flash on terrible photo!

Photographer   Beautiful! I got it! Enjoy the rest of your day,/ I'm Ricardo, I'll come find you at the hotel later.

Tomas   Thank you, thank you very much Harry, that was just a scam.

Harry   What?

Tomas   If any more photographers/ come up to us, just say no thanks maybe tomorrow?

Ebba   Just ignore them next time Harry.

Vera   It's obviously a scam.

Harry   I didn't know.

Ebba   It's fine.

Harry   So why's everyone making a big deal of it?

Vera   Oh my God we've been here two minutes and already he's having a tantrum.

Harry   Shut up! Vera!

Vera   You shut up!

Harry *pushes* **Vera** *over.*

Vera   AOW!

Vera *tries to kick* **Harry** *back.*

Tomas   Hey hey/ hey!

Harry   Get off me!

Harry *throws himself at* **Vera** – *it's a fight.*

Tomas   What is wrong with you?

Ebba   Vera! Vera!

Vera   Ow! Get off!

Harry   AAAAOOO! You get off! She bit me!

Vera   I didn't bite you I pinched/ you stop being such a baby.

Ebba   Don't/ pinch people Vera!

Vera   He started/ it!

Tomas   Stop it. Stop it! Everyone! We're on holiday, we're meant to be having a nice time. What the hell is wrong with you? Hey? Harry. I'm talking to you.

Beat.

Harry. What is wrong with you?

Harry   YOU STARTED IT.

Tomas   HARRY.

Ebba   Tomas.

Signals to leave it.

Tomas   I'm just asking him a question. What?

More signals.

What?

Ebba   Don't shout at him.

Tomas   I'm not shouting. Am I shouting?

Ebba   We haven't eaten all day.

Tomas   Everyone wanted to ski that's not my fault./ I wanted to eat but everyone wanted to ski.

Ebba   I'm not saying . . . I'm just saying no wonder he's like this. We haven't eaten all day.

Tomas   Fine then let's eat.

Ebba   OK.

Tomas   Let's eat. There's a place at the top of the ski lift. Is that going to calm things down? Everyone in agreement with that plan? Don't want to disrupt things if you two have got more plans to attack each other, maybe you want to eat each other?

Vera   I'm starving.

Tomas   Harry?

Harry *nods.*

Ebba   Come on my boy.

Ebba *leads* **Harry** *off, followed by* **Vera**. *Leaving* **Tomas** *on the mountainside alone with all the equipment.*

Tomas   I'll get these then.

Nothing from the exiting family.

'Thanks Dad, that would be great we really appreciate everything you do for us,' 'Oh thanks guys thanks for noticing' 'No problem Dad'.

A Gazex tubes boom and he startles, dropping the equipment. He looks to the mountain and its latent power. **Tomas** *picks up all the equipment and scrambles after them.*

Scene Two

The Outdoor Restaurant

In their skiing gear, the family are sat around a table on a veranda overlooking the top of the mountain surrounded by a family of four, two couples and two **Waiting Staff**.

A **Waitress** *comes and delivers their meals.*

Tomas *is looking at his phone.*

Ebba   Not bad for a first day huh guys?

Harry   After this I'm trying out poles.

Ebba   They're quite big you know.

Vera   He's too small.

Harry   I'm not!

Ebba   Vera. How about next route you can try mine, see how it feels?

Harry   I'm not too small.

Ebba   Tomas.

Tomas   Hm?

Tomas *gets the message, puts his phone away.*

Harry *picks it up.*

Tomas   Where's this food then?

Ebba   It's been long enough now.

Vera   Can you ask them how much longer it's gonna be?

Ebba   I'll see if I can get his attention.

Harry   I bet they've forgotten our order.

Tomas   Probably the altitude up here playing havoc with their/ me-erci beaucoup.

Waitress arrives with their food.

Ebba   Merci beaucoup!

Tomas   Merci beaucoup! Merci, Harry, give me the phone now. Harry.

Harry *hands the phone over.*

Vera   Merci beaucoup.

They start to eat their lunch.

Tomas   That looks great.

Ebba   It really is. It's delicious. Try it.

Ebba *feeds* **Tomas** *some of her food with her fork.*

Tomas   Mm . . . That's really delicious. Harry slow down. What is that dressing?

Ebba   I think it's anchovy or –

Vera   This is so good.

Ebba   Something . . . I can't quite.

Vera   Is there any parmesan?

Loud BOOM! from the Gazex tubes! Everyone startles! Now that they're closer to the top, the explosions sound much louder.

All diners turn to the mountain. In the distance an avalanche starts to fall making the curtains flap.

Tomas *gets his phone out and starts filming.*

Ebba   What was that? Was that an avalanche?

Tomas   Yeah but it's controlled. Wow. Look at that power.

Ebba   Look at that.

Tomas   See they set off an explosion at the top and it moves all the recent snowfall safely before it builds up.

Vera   So it's like a bomb going off?

Tomas   Yeah.

Ebba   Just incredible.

Pause.

Ebba   It's safe isn't it?

Tomas   Yeah yeah, they know what they're doing. Look at that!

Ebba   Where does it stop?

Tomas   I don't know, but they must know how to judge it.

Pause.

I've never seen one this close before you are so lucky kids.

Harry   It doesn't look like it's going to stop.

Vera   Where does it stop? Shouldn't there be like some/
barrier or something.

Pause.

Ebba   That doesn't look controlled to me Tomas that
doesn't look controlled.

Ebba, **Vera** *and* **Harry** *stand up, along with a number of diners.*

Vera   It's not stopping it's gonna hit us.

Harry   It's not stopping!/ DAD! IT'S GONNA HIT US.

Harry *tries to get out of his seat,* **Tomas** *restrains him.*

Tomas   Harry Harry Harry, it's fine it's fine they know what
they're doing. They know what they're doing.

Vera   DAD!/ IT'S NOT STOPPING!

It's closer.

Tomas   VERA IT'S FINE.

Harry   DAD!

It's on them!

Tomas   AHAAHHAAA!!

Mass panic! Everyone scrambles for their lives, **Ebba** *grabs* **Vera**
and **Harry**!

Screaming **Tomas** *grabs his phone and runs, pushing people out of
the way!*

The RUMBLE is almost unbearable!

SCREAMS!!!

The stage and audience are covered in white powder.

And then it's over.

White everywhere.

Long silence.

People cough.

Man   Ça va? Tu vas bien?

Ebba   Um uh . . .

Man   Ça va? Are you OK?

Ebba   Is it safe?

Man   It's safe to come up now. It's safe.

Ebba   Are you sure?

Man   I'm sure. It's safe to come up now.

Ebba   What happened?

Man   Avalanche smoke. It's just avalanche smoke. The avalanche stopped and the smoke it keeps coming.

Ebba *and* **Vera** *slowly stand up,* **Harry** *comes up from under the table, seeing everyone is OK, the* **Man** *moves on.*

Ebba   Are you OK?

Vera   Yeah.

Man (*to other diners*)   Ça va? It is safe now.

Ebba   We're fine. Everything's fine.

Diners start to return to their seats.

Harry   That was scary.

Ebba   Everyone's OK, we're all OK. It's over now. It's over.

Silence.

Vera   Where's Dad? Mum? Where's Dad?

Pause.

Ebba   Just sit down Vera.

Vera   My chair's got stuff all over it.

Ebba *starts to beat their chairs clean with her napkin.*

As she does so, **Harry** *and* **Vera** *look all around the restaurant looking for* **Tomas***.*

Filing in behind several returning diners, **Tomas** *finally appears.*

Tomas   Wow.

Beat.

Damn that was.

Beat.

Whooo!

Beat.

Are you OK? Everyone OK?

Tomas *is laughing.*

That was crazy. They know what they're doing. But that was . . .

Tomas *is laughing.*

Silence from the family.

Phew!

Tomas *looks around and chuckles.*

He looks around again. Lots of people are returning to their seats and returning to their meals, no-one is singling him out.

Tomas   Ah . . .

Tomas *picks up his knife and fork and starts eating his meal again, no-one else can eat.*

Ebba*'s eyes are on stalks.*

Tomas   Mm . . . it's good. You want to try?

He offers **Ebba** *a fork.*

Ebba *is too much in shock to react.*

Tomas   No?

Silence from **Ebba**, *he puts his fork down. Maybe he can't eat after all.*

Tomas   Ahhh . . .

Tomas *looks out to the landscape.*

More silence.

Tomas   And here comes the sun.

Long silence.

Lights down.

Scene Three

The Mountain

The family are on the mountain.

Tomas   How about we do this run and then go get some hot chocolate? How about that? Guys?

Little enthusiasm.

Tomas   Everyone ready?

Ebba   Tomas, I'm not sure anyone wants to ski anymore.

Tomas   Course they do, it's what we're here for right? Skiing. Vera? Harry?

Ebba   We can head back to the room if you want.

Tomas   Yeah we can do that if you want?

Vera   I want to go back.

Harry   Me too.

Tomas   That's fine. Let's go back. I don't mind. Sure
no-one wants a hot chocolate? I think we've earned it after
today!

Vera and **Harry** *walk off leaving their kit behind followed by* **Ebba**.

Tomas   No, OK. I'll get these don't worry.

Tomas *starts to gather the kit up.*

Meanwhile **Ebba** *and the kids have been approached by . . .*

Photographer   Mrs . . . here I have your photos.

Ebba   Ah, OK. Uh . . . not now thank you . . .

Photographer   I have prints. . .

Photographer *gets out photos from a folder.*

Ebba   Oh OK . . .

Photographer   Yes.

Ebba   I'm just trying to . . .

Photographer   Yes? See.

Ebba   OK. OK. Thanks. Yes. These are. Yes. They're great.

Photographer   Handsome boy. Heartbreaker.

Ebba   Yes.

Photographer   One minute a baby and then . . .

Ebba   Yes.

Photographer   Beautiful family. Happy memories.

Tomas *appears and watches* **Ebba**. **Ebba** *flicks away from the
group shot.*

Ebba   I'll take this one and this one.

Photographer   And this one? All four family?

Ebba   Just those thank you.

Photographer   D'accord. This and this. That is fifty-two Euro. Seventy cents.

Ebba   Oh. Um. Right.

Ebba *gets her purse out.*

She hands him some notes.

Ebba   OK thank you.

Photographer   That's not enough.

Ebba   Sorry.

She hands him another note before trying to leave.

Photographer   Still not enough.

She hands some more notes.

Photographer   No.

She gets some more out.

Ebba   Look just just take it.

The **Photographer** *seems to be deciding rather than counting.*

Photographer   Your change./ I have some change in my.

Ebba   No thank you it's fine.

The **Photographer** *leaves.*

Tomas   All OK? Are those the photos?

Ebba   Yeah.

Tomas   Let me see.

Beat.

That it?

Beat.

Ebba   I didn't like myself in the others.

Tomas   Bet you looked great.

Ebba   No.

Tomas   That's ridiculous.

Ebba   I didn't like it.

Tomas   You always look great in photos it's me that spoils them.

Ebba *starts to walk to join the kids,* **Tomas** *runs alongside her.*

Tomas   I don't know. I might be wrong but, you seem, irritated.

Ebba   OK.

Tomas   OK.

Ebba   OK.

Tomas   Right. So. Well. Are you? Irritated.

Beat.

Ebba   No. No I don't think so.

Tomas   OK great. That's/ great I was

Ebba   Should I be?

Pause.

Tomas   No I. No, I don't *think* so.

Ebba   No?

Tomas *exhales as if wracking his brain.*

Tomas   Hm . . . No. I. No. I can't.

Ebba   OK then.

Ebba *carries on walking.*

Tomas   OK then. Yeah.

Beat.

Ebba.

Beat.

Maybe. I was just thinking maybe we should take them straight back let's not worry about a hot chocolate? I think they're a bit tired. Harry looks tired.

Ebba   Yup OK. Do it.

Ebba *invites* **Tomas** *to catch up with the kids.*

Tomas *is unsure what to do,* **Ebba** *maintains the invite . . . an anxious* **Tomas** *runs after the kids.*

Tomas   Kids let's just head back I think everyone needs a rest.

Harry   Is everything OK?

Tomas   What?

Vera   What's going on? With Mum.

Tomas   Nothing.

Harry   Were you two arguing?

Tomas   No.

Vera   What was that about?

Tomas   Nothing we were just talking.

Harry   Why does she look upset then?

Tomas   Look I know your mum better than anyone else. She's not upset. OK?

Unconvinced, **Harry** *and* **Vera** *exit.*

On **Tomas** *looking back to* **Ebba** – *yeah, she looks upset.*

Lights down.

Scene Four

Hotel Suite

Vera *is sat on the floor looking at her iPad.*

Ebba *is holding* **Harry**'s *pyjamas.*

Harry   LEAVE ME ALONE!

Ebba   Come on Harry.

Harry   NO LEAVE ME ALONE! GO AWAY!

Ebba   Harry.

Tomas   Harry I don't like your tone of voice; you can't speak to your mother like that.

Harry   I DON'T WANT TO GO TO BED. YOU CAN'T TELL ME WHAT TO DO.

Ebba *tries to pull* **Harry**'s *top off.*

Ebba   It's/ bedtime.

Harry   NO! GET OFF ME! LEAVE ME ALONE!

Tomas *tries to grab* **Harry**, *but* **Harry** *kicks out violently and screams.*

Harry   AHHHAAAAAHAHAHAHA!! NO!/ NO! NO! NOOOOOOOO!

Tomas   Stop it! Stop it! Stop it! Harry! You have to go to bed you're eight years old.

Ebba   No no no no/ Harry Harry Harry.

Vera   Just leave him alone!/ God! He doesn't want to go to bed we're on holiday let him stay up! What does any of this achieve?

Ebba   He has to go to bed, we've had a very long day, and he's tired. We're all tired.

Tomas   Yeah.

Vera   He's not.

Ebba   He is.

Vera   He doesn't look it.

Ebba   He's tired.

Harry   I'm not. Look.

Ebba   Harry.

Tomas   Harry.

Ebba   We're all going to bed soon. Can you talk to him?/ He has to go to bed?

Vera   This is *not* my problem./ None of this is my problem don't drag me into it.

Tomas   Well unfortunately we're a family and we're all staying in this room/ so it is your problem as well Vera. We all need to

Vera   I didn't want to come here, I wanted to go to St Tropez/ but no-one ever listens to me in this family we could be on a beach right now rather than dealing with this.

Ebba   Oh Vera/ this is not the time to make this about you.

Harry *gets* **Tomas'** *phone and starts watching something on it.*

Tomas   Harry /we're trying to talk as a family.

Vera   No of course it's never/ about me is it? That's exactly my point it is literally *never* about me in this family. It's Dad, then Harry then you, then the dog, then me.

Ebba   Yes, I'm an awful/ mother Vera, you're the victim I'm sorry for bringing you to the Alps on holiday.

Harry   I want to FaceTime Lena.

Tomas   We are not FaceTiming the dog. Harry. Give me the phone. Harry. Harry.

Harry *ignores him.*

Tomas   HARRY.

Vera   DON'T SHOUT/ AT HIM LIKE THAT.

Tomas   I'm *trying*/ to get him to listen.

Vera   OH MY GOD!/ You two.

Tomas   Ve/ ra.

Ebba   Watch/ your attitude Vera I am sick of being spoken to as if I'm some maid!

Vera   Just go!/ He doesn't want you in here! I don't want you in here! Why don't you just go?

Tomas   This is *our* hotel suite!/ We've only got one living room!

Harry   Can I have your phone Mum?

Vera   Well pay for a pod for us then?/ Then we can all have some peace and quiet.

Tomas   We've got two rooms! I'm not paying for a pod for you guys on top of paying for us to have a family suite/ I'm not doing it.

Harry   Mum./ Can I have your phone?

Vera   Fine well this is what you get.

Tomas   Maybe we just need to figure out how to all get on better here and we can start by you two doing as you're told. Harry go to bed and Vera drop the attitude.

Vera   Sure/ yeah whatever.

Harry   Vera give/ me your phone.

Vera   GET OFF!/ MUM! Tell him! MUM!

Tomas   HARRY! LET GO!

Vera   TELL HIM!

Ebba   Harry! Harry stop it! HARRY! Can we just. Can we just stop shouting please? Can we talk about this without everyone shouting?

Silence.

Thank you. I know you're angry,/ but let's all just take a deep breath.

Vera   I thought he needed to go to bed and I had a bad attitude? Make up your mind. He's either got to go to bed, or he hasn't. You can't keep changing what's best for us to suit you.

Ebba   Vera.

Vera   Why don't *you* go to bed and leave us in here? Shut the door. I don't care.

Ebba   We're not doing that.

Vera   Then why not go somewhere else? Leave your phone for him and go somewhere else? It's a big hotel. He won't pay for a pod, we can't go anywhere else, so why don't you two, give us some space. And when he's ready, he'll go to bed.

Ebba   Can't/ we –

Vera   I don't want to talk anymore.

Ebba *does not want to leave it like this.*

Tomas   Maybe we should . . .

Ebba   What?

Tomas   Maybe we should give them some space . . .

Vera   Finally.

Ebba   Vera, I really don't like your tone/ you are really pushing your luck.

Vera   I'M NOT SAYING ANYTHING, YOU'RE THE ONE WHO DRAGGED ME INTO THIS I DON'T CARE

WHAT TIME HE GOES TO BED I DON'T CARE ABOUT
ANY OF THIS I JUST WANT TO BE LEFT ALONE.

Harry Mum can I have your phone?

Defeated **Ebba** *hands* **Harry** *her phone.*

Tomas Come on give them some space.

Ebba I don't think it's a good idea they're upset.

Tomas Give them some space, Vera you're in charge. (*Off*
Ebba.) Let's let her get on with it. We'll be downstairs. We'll
be downstairs if there's any problems just ring.

Vera Whatever.

Ebba *bridles.*

Harry *climbs back on to the bed with* **Ebba**'s *phone.*

Tomas *and* **Ebba** *step out –* **Harry** *and* **Vera** *go into darkness.*

Tomas *and* **Ebba** *look at each other.*

Tomas This is what happens when you raise strong
independent children. You get thrown out of your own
room!

Tomas *can't help but laugh.*

They both look out to the mountain.

The Gazex tubes boom.

Ebba I need a drink.

Tomas Let's get a drink. And dinner. Come on.

Lights down.

Scene Five

Hotel Restaurant

Tomas *and* **Ebba** *are sat with* **Charlotte** *and* **Brady**.

Tomas   So, how was your day?

Charlotte   Um, it was fantastic, right? We had a great day. I met this one, I mean. (*Pointing to* **Brady**.) Yeah.

Tomas   Yeah?

Charlotte   We bumped into each other this morning in the queue to the lift. And, er, I guess we were both longing for someone.

Laughs all around.

No, I'm just kidding. No, we had a great day and we had a good time snowboarding and hanging out, talking it was, it was great. Really nice. You told me that you're very religious . . .

Brady   I did not/ say that.

Charlotte   Yes, you did.

Brady   Not that I'm/ *very* religious, no that's not what I said.

Charlotte   Yeah you did. It's alright. What's wrong with that? Don't be ashamed,/ own it.

Brady   I'm not ashamed! Well, allow me to explain, I told this one . . .

Charlotte   Excuse me?

Brady   . . . That I'm not an atheist which is/ very different.

Charlotte   Who the fuck is this one?

Pause.

Tomas   You said it before.

Charlotte   Did I? (*Remembering.*) I met 'this one'.

Brady   Just a joke.

Charlotte   Oh yeah.

Laughter.

Brady   Anyway, did you guys brave the crowds today?

Ebba   Yeah, we did. Yeah. It was . . . well . . .

Ebba *takes a big swig of wine.*

Laughter.

Tomas   Yeah, it was great it was great. We skied all morning and then we . . . Well.

We actually we uh, we did a little bit more in the afternoon but went home because we had. Well we had a sort of crazy experience actually. Um . . .

Ebba *laughs.* **Tomas** *looks to* **Ebba** *for a shared connection.* **Ebba** *avoids his eye.*

Charlotte   OK.

Tomas   Yeah. So we were sitting at the top restaurant, you know the top one, with the magnificent view.

Charlotte   Yeah,/ it's a nice bar there.

Brady   I haven't been there yet, but everyone keeps saying it's magnificent.

Charlotte   I'll take you tomorrow.

Brady   OK! Sorry. Carry on, you were at the top restaurant.

Tomas   Yeah, we were at the top restaurant, and we had uh well we saw an avalanche, didn't we?

Ebba *giggles before taking another big swig of wine.*

Brady   An avalanche?/ Holy shit!

Charlotte   Really?

Tomas   Yeah it was. It was this/ sort of incredible

Ebba *laughs uncontrollably.*

Tomas   What?

Ebba   Ignore me. Sorry. Ignore me.

Ebba *pours herself a mighty glass of wine.*

Polite laughter.

Tomas   Anyway, so we were sitting there, and it was a controlled/ avalanche, so it was . . .

Brady   Controlled avalanche, yeah.

Tomas   But quite quickly it grew kind of big. It was like. It just kept getting bigger and bigger and, I've never really seen such a big avalanche, and I was like, er, for a moment it looked like it was going to smash into the restaurant. It was kind of terrifying.

Brady   Wow.

Charlotte   But you're OK? It didn't hit the restaurant did it?

Tomas   No, but for a moment . . . it looked like it would. When I talk about it look, I'm getting goose bumps.

Tomas *shows off the goose bumps on his arm to* **Ebba** *who is still smirking.*

Charlotte   What did you do?

Tomas   I mean, there wasn't much anyone could do, you're on the mountain/ it's you know it's split second stuff

Ebba   It was horrifying actually. Utterly horrifying.

Pause.

Charlotte   You all had a fright?

Ebba   Yeah, we did.

Tomas   Yeah,/ it's one of those –

Brady   And the kids are alright? Are they OK?

Tomas   Yeah, everyone is fine. Everyone is fine thank God. We got shaken up you know, you (Ebba) got a bit afraid, didn't you? But really it was

Ebba *laughs at this. . .*

Tomas   . . . But I mean it wasn't . . . It was controlled, and they know what they're doing/ it was just in the moment you think –

Ebba   He got so scared that he ran away from the table.

Brady *laughs.*

Tomas   What? No,/ I didn't.

Brady   You ran?

Ebba   Yeah, he did.

Tomas   No, I didn't. No. No. No.

Beat.

Ebba   Come on.

Tomas   No. No. No. No. No.

Ebba   You ran away from the table.

Tomas   What? No, I did not.

Ebba   . . .

Tomas   I did not.

Ebba   When it came at us, you ran away.

Tomas   No, I didn't . . . I most certainly/ did not do that.

Ebba   You grabbed your phone and your gloves and ran like hell.

Tomas   Please . . . I did no such thing. I did no such thing.

Ebba   Well. You did.

Tomas   That's not how I remember it.

Tomas *laughs, no-one is quite sure whether to laugh or not.*

Ebba   You ran away.

Ebba *takes another drink of wine.*

Tomas   Ebba, please. I didn't do that. It's weird./ I think we're still a little shaken up by the whole thing. It's not even possible to run in ski boots.

Charlotte   It sounds awful. Really a horrible thing to go through.

Ebba (*laughing to herself*)   Can't run in ski boots? Can you not run in ski boots?

Tomas thinks you can't run in ski boots now and I imagined the whole thing. Unbelievable.

Brady   Well. Maybe . . .

Charlotte   But isn't this one of those situations that kind of comes really quick? And none of us know how we'd react. How do you know how to react?

Brady   I don't know.

Ebba   You can run in ski boots.

Tomas   They're not supple enough.

Ebba   Can you run in ski boots?

Brady (*pause*)   You know, I haven't been skiing in years so I'm really not the person to ask about these things.

Tomas' *pride is wounded.*

Charlotte   'About these things.' You are so cute! Isn't he so cute?

Charlotte *gives* **Brady** *a patronising kiss.*

Ebba *laughs.*

Tomas *tries to join in, but his pride is too injured.*

Lights down.

Scene Six

Hotel Corridor

Ebba *walks along with the room key;* **Tomas** *runs after her.*

Tomas   Ebba!

Beat.

Ebba!

Ebba   What?

Tomas   Can we just stop for a second? Ebba? Stop! Please.

Ebba *stops.*

Tomas   Thank you.

Ebba   Why won't admit what happened?

Tomas   Well . . .

Beat.

Pff. Because, that's not how I see,/ what happened.

Ebba   How do you see what happened? Hm? How?

Tomas   I see, what happened. And it's just not what you see.

Ebba   This is so weird, this is so weird.

Tomas   What's so weird about it?

Ebba   Admit what you did!

Tomas   I can't 'admit' to your perception. That's not how I see it. I just. I really can't relate to your description of things. And the way you tried to convince everybody at dinner that your version was the truth . . . It was just really hard on me.

Ebba It was hard for me, hearing you deny it.

Tomas I'm sure. It must be hard for you. I don't want that for you. I don't want that for either of us. I want us to be – like we always are. We're a team.

Ebba I didn't recognize us at all. I didn't recognize you ... or myself.

Tomas I didn't recognize you either.

Ebba I don't want us to be like that, this is meant to be our family holiday and we're disagreeing like that at dinner/ it's so embarrassing.

Tomas I don't want it to be like this. I don't ever want to have a dinner like that again.

Ebba Me neither. I hated it. It's not good . . .

Tomas That's not us.

Ebba That's not us.

Tomas No.

Ebba We're normally so . . .

Tomas Together on everything. Co-pilots.

Ebba Right.

Tomas We're a team, so let's make sure we get back there and put all this behind us.

Ebba OK.

Tomas OK. Great. Phew!

Ebba OK.

Tomas Great.

Ebba Look. Try to hug me . . . I need one.

Tomas So, do I.

They hug.

Tomas' *phone starts to ring.* **Ebba** *tries to disengage.* **Tomas** *doesn't let her.*

Tomas   Ignore it. Ignore it.

It carries on ringing, eventually **Ebba** *can't ignore it.*

Tomas *quickly turns it off and puts his arms around* **Ebba** *again for a hug.*

Ebba *disengages.*

Ebba   Sorry, I can't. I just. I can't get past/ the whole

Tomas   Come on Ebba.

Ebba   No, it's actually really important for us for the kids that we agree on things like this otherwise it's going to chip away at us.

Tomas   We just said we'd put it behind us.

Ebba   We need to have a shared vision/ of this or it's

Tomas   You do know it's actually impossible for us to share the same perspective on things. Scientifically.

Ebba   What?

Tomas   It's science. It's impossible for us to see the same thing so/ we're going to diverge at some –

Ebba   But there are you know – Observable facts we should be able to agree on.

Tomas   Are there?

Ebba   Tomas.

Tomas   Really? I don't know.

Ebba   Come on. And seeing us united and in agreement on things is good for the kids. It's good for us as a couple, that we find a way to agree on things. It's good for us to make sure that we're not at odds on stuff.

Tomas   OK. So, what exactly are you trying to say? What do you want me to say? Because I don't know any more.

*The **Cleaner** enters dragging a reluctant vacuum cleaner. He slowly walks past them. They wait patiently for privacy.*

Ebba   We had lunch at the top restaurant.

Pause.

Tomas   OK, agreed.

Ebba   We were all there.

Pause.

Tomas   Yes, we were all there.

Beat.

Ebba   An avalanche happened?

Tomas   An avalanche happened.

Beat.

Ebba   We . . . were all terrified.

Beat.

Ebba   And?

Thomas   And.

Beat.

Ebba   And that's, it. Everyone was ok.

Tomas   That's what we say happened?

Ebba   Well, that's all we can agree/ on. So, I guess

Tomas   I'm totally OK with that. Totally OK with that. If I knew if that's – if I knew that's what you meant. Sorry. I thought. OK, if that's what you mean. That's our – that's fine. I'm totally fine with that.

Ebba   OK.

Tomas   OK.

Ebba   So, we have a unified front.

Tomas   Hooray! Yes, I am totally fine with that spin on things.

Ebba   All right, then.

Tomas   Alright then deal.

Tomas *offers a hand,* **Ebba** *shakes it.*

Tomas   Whooo! That's a relief.

Ebba   We experienced an avalanche. And it was scary.

Tomas   Christ . . . We're on holiday. We shouldn't be acting like this. Let's put all this behind us. There was an avalanche, we were terrified, but everyone's fine. OK? Job done.

Ebba   OK.

Tomas (*bold!*)   On with the holiday!

Scene Seven

Hotel Bathroom

Tomas *and* **Ebba** *get ready for bed, brushing teeth in a rehearsed, silent fashion. She pushes the toilet seat down and finds herself glowering at* **Tomas***.*

Outside the controlled explosions from the Gazex tubes continue.

Tomas *heads into the room leaving* **Ebba** *alone in the bathroom.*

It's not over.

Scene Eight

Hotel Room

The family is getting kitted up.

Ebba   Harry . . . Your other glove is over there, over by Daddy. Here.

Harry   What?

Ebba   The other one's/ over there, next to Dad.

Harry   I can't find my goggles.

Ebba   Where did you put them?

Harry   I don't know./ I can't ski without my goggles.

Tomas   They'll be in here somewhere,/ just take a look.

Harry   I'm not going/ without them.

Tomas   Ebba/ have you seen his goggles?

Ebba   Where did you take them off last?

Harry   I don't know.

Tomas   Well think.

Harry   I don't know.

Tomas   When you came in last night what did you do with them?

Harry   I DON'T REMEMBER.

Ebba *steps back from the fray.*

Tomas   Hey hey it's OK. We'll find it. You know Mummy is the master of finding things. And then, we can all go and enjoy a day on the slopes. Right? Right Vera? Vera.

Silence from **Vera.**

Tomas   'Yes Dad. I can't wait.' Me neither Vera.

Ebba *stares at her family.*

Ebba   You know, I was thinking about skiing all by myself today.

Tomas *guffaws.*

Tomas   What? Really?

Ebba   Yes.

Tomas *looks at the kids,* **Vera** *totally disengaged,* **Harry** *furiously turning the place upside down looking for his goggles.*

Tomas   Well . . .

Ebba   I think I'd like to ski on my own today. Unless that's a problem?

Tomas   Uh, No, no . . .

Ebba   Do I hear a 'but'?

Tomas (*beat*)   No, go ahead. OK. We'll catch you later. We'll catch you later. Maybe meet for lunch or something?

Harry   What? Where are we going for lunch? We're not going to that place, again are we?

Tomas   No, no I'm just saying we'll meet for lunch that's all I didn't say where.

Harry   Who are we meeting?

Tomas   Mummy. We're meeting Mummy for lunch.

Harry   Why are we meeting Mummy where's she going?

Tomas   Mummy wants to ski on her own today.

Harry   What? Why? What's the point in that?

Tomas *is lost for words.*

Ebba   I just. Feel like it.

Silence.

Vera *guffaws.*

Ebba   Vera? Anything you want to add?

Vera   No.

Ebba   What's so funny about me wanting to ski on my own?

Vera   Why'd you feel like it?

Ebba   I can have a day skiing on my own,/ it's no big –

Tomas   Yeah, it's fine./ It's cool.

Vera   You've never done it before.

Ebba *laughs*.

Ebba   I'm only going for a ski on my own.

Harry   What's the point in that?

Ebba   Harry! Sometimes! Mummies . . . They./ You know

Tomas   Mummies need a bit of 'me time'.

Ebba   Yeah/ 'me time'.

Harry   Why? We're on holiday.

Vera   Oh my God.

Ebba   Harry. Everyone does it OK? Every family lets their mums get away now and again. It's healthy.

Tomas   Yeah and their daddies too./ Sometimes.

Vera   Do *kids* ever get 'me time'?

Tomas   All of your time is me time Vera. That's why Mummy and I need 'me time'.

Harry   I don't want to ski without you.

Harry *pulls off his glove*.

Ebba   Can you? (deal with this)

Tomas *heads to* **Harry**.

Tomas   Yeah, it's fine it's fine we'll be fine. Take my credit card.

Tomas *opens his wallet.* **Ebba** *makes for the door.*

Ebba   No, I'll use my own thank you.

Ebba *leaves.*

Tomas   Alright! Another day on the slopes!

Vera *puts her headphones on.*

Harry   WHERE IS SHE GOING?

Tomas' *shoulders sink.*

Lights down.

Scene Nine

The Mountain

Movement sequence as **Ebba** *skis alone.*

She tries to enjoy it, but something isn't quite working for her.

Eventually she gives up.

Lights down.

Scene Ten

Café

Ebba *sits facing* **Charlotte** *who is coyly waving to a hunk at the bar, in a café with big glass windows.*

Charlotte   He has a lot of huskies. Italian. Very little English. Which is a good thing I think.

Ebba   Is it?

Charlotte   He speaks as much as a woman needs.

Ebba *laughs.*

Ebba   Well, that's the truth.

Charlotte   What's it like out there today?

Ebba   Good. I've been on my own today.

Charlotte   But I thought this was a *family* holiday? 'Time to focus.' Not as much fun as you thought?

Ebba   I didn't really enjoy skiing on my own this morning.

Charlotte   Then you need company.

Ebba   You seem to have had a lot of men.

Beat.

Sorry.

Charlotte   I guess that's right. Yeah . . .

Ebba   Do you have some kind of arrangement with your husband or boyfriend?

Charlotte   No way! We each take responsibility for our relationships and keep it at that. Seems to work out pretty well.

Beat.

You look surprised.

Ebba   Well, yeah . . . Aren't you ever jealous? And what about him?

Charlotte   If he has a good time with some woman, why shouldn't I let him have it?

Ebba   You actually mean that? That you're happy he's with someone else?

Charlotte   Sure, I'm happy for him; I love him.

Waiter *returns with* **Ebba**'s *coffee.* **Waiter** *leaves.*

Ebba   What if you meet someone and, you don't want to go back to the family?

Charlotte   I always go back. You're worried you wouldn't?

Beat.

Ebba   OK. To a certain extent, I understand. You're still young and attractive. . . But aren't you afraid of being alone, being left? What if he falls in love with one of these women, what if one of these women are younger than you? What if he can't stop thinking about her when he's with you, and you're just the boring domestic part of his life, and with her it's all fun and sexy and no responsibility. Isn't that just – Aren't you both risking your whole family and risking messing up your children's lives?

Charlotte   I suppose.

Ebba   What if he leaves you?

Charlotte   Well, of course I don't want to be left alone. But there are lots of people who are important in my life, not just my husband and my children. I can't go building my entire self-esteem on being a woman in a relationship or being a mother. I don't need him to feel safe.

Ebba *doesn't feel safe with* **Tomas**.

Ebba   OK, I get that, I'm all – (*Fist pump.*) but does it actually work? *Actually* does it work? Like are you *100 per cent* sure no one gets hurt?

Charlotte   What can I say?

Ebba   Are you sure that it doesn't hurt your children? Like how can you know, they aren't picking up on the fact that you two aren't straight with each other, or not 100 per cent invested in each other. My kids they can spot the slightest bit of disagreement between me and Tomas a mile off. They have a radar for it. How can you be sure your kids aren't (messed up)?

Charlotte   What?

Ebba   How can you be sure you're not screwing up your kids by being so selfish?

Beat.

I'm sorry I don't mean to judge. I just want to know how it works. For you.

Charlotte   There's someone else?

Ebba *is disturbed by her own transparency.*

Ebba   No.

Charlotte   Are you sure?

Ebba   Yes.

Beat.

Yes.

Beat.

I'm sure.

Beat.

OK nothing's happened/ but there is someone.

Charlotte   But something could, if you let yourself.

Ebba   There is someone a work colleague and there's. I think there's . . . a connection there. I know there is but nothing's happened.

I've never spoken about this with anyone.

Charlotte   Would you like something to happen?

Ebba   No. I. I think about what it might be like. Sometimes. Often. When he's . . . near. But nothing's happened and it won't happen.

Charlotte   But you'd like it to.

Charlotte *drinks some coffee.*

Ebba   I just couldn't bear it if something I did, hurt the kids. Something silly and selfish, hurt the kids and Tomas. And changed things forever.

Charlotte   I think raising kids in an unhappy relationship is the quickest way to screw up your kids actually. The best thing I can do for them is be happy. Are your kids doing fine?

Beat.

OK.

Ebba   You don't – Relationships aren't just – you know – there are ups and downs and you have to work at them. You know; building a relationship with another person, spending your life together, getting married, having kids, that's worth so much more than tumbling around with a young colleague or some Italian/ at some

Charlotte   Gorgeous Italian.

Ebba   Gorgeous Italian at some ski resort in France. You have to see that right?

Charlotte   I do.

Beat.

But why do we have to choose? In this day and age. Why do we have to choose? Who says we have to choose? Who says? I say, we can have both. We can have long-term and short-term relationships. Whatever our needs are, we should be allowed to meet them.

Ebba   I can't imagine that working for me.

Charlotte   Because you, like most women, believe what you believe. And you work at your relationships, and every now and again you're rewarded with a few weeks or a month or two of peace and happiness where the resentment dissipates for a while. And then you're unhappy again. You're lonely again. You retreat into your fantasies with a friend and open yourself up to the attention he gives you, and that gives you enough of a boost to go back to shovelling in the endless trenches of your unhappy relationship. Doing all the emotional labour, on your own so that you can hold it together for the benefit of everyone else, except you. I refuse that deal. Maybe you should too.

Ebba   The thing/ I can't . . .

Charlotte *spies a new man in the distance.*

Charlotte   Would you? Would you excuse me. . .

Ebba   Sure sure go ahead. Go ahead.

Charlotte *heads over to the new man at another table.*

Alone, **Ebba** *looks on.*

She looks out of the window and startles when she sees **Tomas**, **Vera** *and* **Harry** *in the full skiing kit walking outside towards the gondola platform.* **Vera** *storming ahead,* **Harry** *behind and* **Tomas** *struggling to keep up with the equipment.*

Through the glass **Ebba** *watches her family.*

She puts her hand on the window but doesn't draw their attention.

Scene Eleven

Gondola Lift Platform

Tomas   Vera. Vera? Stop!

Beat.

Can you give me a hand with this stuff?

They stop and **Vera** *takes some equipment from* **Tomas**.

Tomas *takes a glove off and checks his phone.*

Tomas   Oh, Mats and his new girlfriend Jenny have arrived. OK. So, what do you guys want to do next?

Harry   I want to try snowboarding on a red run./ Can we
do snowboarding next?

Tomas   OK Vera. How about you?

Beat.

Vera. What do you want to do? Vera.

Vera   I want to go home.

Tomas   Ha. What?

Beat.

You're not serious.

Beat.

We've only just got here. Aren't you having a good time?

Vera   Are you?

Tomas   Ha! Well. Pff. It's not really about me. This is a
family holiday it's about you guys. I'm not supposed to
enjoy it.

Beat.

Well I am enjoying it. I'm enjoying being with you guys.
Spending time with you. Us all being together.

Vera   We're not all together.

Tomas   Well Mummy needs a break and it's kind to give her
that break.

Vera   Whatever.

Tomas   What does that mean?

Vera   It means, whatever whatever.

Tomas   I don't follow what you mean.

Vera   It means whatever you want to believe, whatever.
Let's just go. I don't care. Let's go.

Tomas   She's just skiing on her own.

Vera   She's not just skiing on her own though is she?

Tomas   Hey your Mum really loves you, both of you.

Vera   I know that.

Beat.

I just don't think she loves you.

Tomas *stops*.

Vera   Do you think she does?

Beat.

So, I'm saying; if you two are gonna get a divorce, then I want to go home.

Harry   What? Are you two getting a divorce? Dad?

Vera   And if we are going home because you two are getting a divorce then I want an iPhone XR in gold.

Harry   Dad! What's going on? Are you getting a divorce? When?

Tomas   No, we are not getting a divorce. Why would you – what – why why – that's no. That's absolutely categorically – OK. Believe me. I *know* I'm your Dad. OK, and I would know. I would know. I'd be the first to, she'd have to, I'd have to give approval of, and you know. I'm not gonna so. Why would you think – has she said something? To make you think that. Has she said something? Or have you overheard something. On the phone. Is that why you is that why you said that?

Vera   No.

Tomas   Well then there's nothing to worry about is there? OK. Guys. Trust me on this.

Vera *walks off*, **Harry** *follows, and* **Tomas** *chases after.*

Tomas   Vera!

Ebba *steps onto the mountain.*

The Gazex tubes boom – she doesn't flinch, she stays on the mountain.

Lights down.

Scene Twelve

Corridor

Mats *and* **Jenny** *fool around at* **Ebba** *and* **Tomas'** *door.*

Jenny   Come on, behave.

Mats   Here, feel this, feel this . . . No one can see us . . .

Jenny   No.

Mats   No-one can see us.

Jenny   Mats!

She indicates the **Cleaner** *walking past, giving them a judgemental stare.*

Mats   Hi.

Eventually the **Cleaner** *leaves and* **Mats** *is immediately all over* **Jenny** *again.*

Jenny   No Mats.

Mats   Come on. Please? Don't be like that come to Papa!

Jenny *rejects him.*

Mats   Why'd you do this to me?

Jenny   Because.

Mats   Now I'm gonna have to see Ebba with a massive throbbing ha/-iii!!

Ebba *opens the door with a glass of wine in her hand.*

Ebba   Hi!/ You must be Jenny, come in come in!

Jenny   Hi!/ So nice to meet you! Mats has told me so much about you guys!

They enter the room where **Tomas** *is opening another bottle of wine.*

Tomas   Here comes trouble!

Mats   Here he is! Been too long.

The two hug.

Tomas   Hi Jenny, you're too good for him!

Mats   Ignore him.

Ebba   The kids are asleep so it's just us, you've been here before, right, Jenny?

Jenny   It's my third season. But it's the first time with Mats. It's been fun, we've had a great time today haven't we?

Mats   Absolutely.

Jenny   How's it been for you guys?

Tomas *yanks out the cork – everyone startles and laughs nervously!*

Ebba *offers her drained glass to* **Tomas** *as she talks.*

Ebba   Well . . . It's been . . . We've had a fantastic time. It's been great. A great place to bring the kids. The conditions are great, all this snow . . . And I had a day of skiing on my own too. You should have that too./ It was great.

Tomas   I'd like that.

Ebba   It's wonderful to go at your own pace and just . . . Maybe. I know, wouldn't it be nice for you boys to ski together again?

Tomas   That would be, cool . . .

Ebba   It must be ages since you skied together!

Tomas   Uh. Yeah it is.

Ebba   I think you should do it.

Tomas   Let's see, maybe see what the kids want to do, they might want to –

Ebba   How about tomorrow? I can take the kids. Don't feel guilty about it.

Tomas   I don't.

Beat.

I was just thinking that this is their holiday/ they might have plans together –

Ebba   I'm sorry . . . I'm sorry. This is your holiday I didn't mean to take control of it, you decide what works for you.

Jenny   No problem.

Ebba   Jeez! What am I like?

Ebba *takes a huge gulp of wine. She is already on another level of drunk than the others.*

Jenny   This wine is *great*.

Ebba   Isn't it? That's the best thing about coming here, whatever wine you buy, you just know you can put away two bottles of it without really realizing, have some more.

Ebba *tops up* **Jenny***'s drink and takes a gulp herself.*

Tomas   So what do you do Jenny? When you're not trying to keep this guy in check.

Mats   Heey! Watch it!

Tomas   I'm always watching it when you're around.

Mats *and* **Tomas** *cackle in a tragic way.*

Tomas   Sorry Jenny, you were saying.

Jenny   I work in a bar.

Silence.

Tomas   OK.

Ebba   That's great!

Beat.

We love bars. We never. We never go. Anymore. We never do anything. But if we did. We would go to a bar. What kind of bar?

Tomas   Do you enjoy it?

Jenny   It's OK I guess. I have a good manager.

Tomas   Well there's plenty of time.

Ebba   Tomas.

Tomas   What?

Ebba   You sound like you're judging.

Tomas   I'm just saying. He's forty-two and he's still figuring out what he wants to do, I can judge him!

Laughter.

Mats   He's judging because actually he wants to be me.

More tragic cackling from **Tomas** *and* **Mats**.

Jenny   I know what I want to do.

Tomas   Oh yeah?

Jenny   Yeah, I want to open a place here.

Ebba   Like a hotel?

Jenny   A bar.

Mats   She has some great ideas. Great ideas. Got it *all* worked out.

Tomas   That's great.

Jenny   I've worked in bars all my life, and I've been coming here for years and it feels like it's missing something with a bit of . . .

Tomas   Qui/ et.

Jenny   Sou/ l.

Tomas   Soul-yeah.

Jenny   Yeah, there's nothing in the evenings for you know, young people. Or people without kids.

Mats   It could do with livening up around here.

Jenny   I was talking to a guy last season.

Mats   What guy who is he where can I kill him?

Tomas *and* **Ebba** *laugh.*

Jenny   They said they were opening a night club. So, I went there and asked if they were hiring. I talked to their head bartender; a guy called Micke. And well, one thing was he was kind of threatening/ to begin with but that's by the by.

Tomas   What?

Mats   What do you mean?

Pause.

Jenny   Well. He what. I don't know what the right word is but it was like he fronted me? Is that what you would say?

Tomas   He was aggressive with you?

Mats   Which bar?

Jenny   The one with the green on the front.

Tomas   What did he say? Do you want us/ to have a word?

Jenny   Yeah. He was all like, 'So, ever worked a bar before?' And I went, 'Yeah, I've worked all over' and I was about to list all the places I'd been and before I could, he like stepped up to me, and looked down and said, 'Are you any good?'

Ebba   We were . . .

Jenny   And his whole body language and demeanour was just sneering like looking down on me as if I was like some kind/ of second-class . . .

Ebba   We were in an avalanche yesterday.

Ebba *drinks her wine.*

Tomas   What was that?

Ebba   I said, we were in an avalanche yesterday.

Mats   You were actually in it? In an avalanche?

Ebba   We're here, so everything's OK. But . . . The thing is . . . we were about to have lunch it had just been served when we heard a loud bang. You hear that all the time around here. I don't like it, but Tomas says it's nothing to worry about. Anyway, everyone at the restaurant turns to have a look. We see the snow start cascading. And I mean, it's spectacular.

Tomas *nods in agreement as if he's a willing participant in this conversation.*

Ebba   People start taking pictures. It's quite . . . impressive. Until we realize that something's wrong because this wall of snow is heading straight towards us.

Mats   It's heading towards you?

Ebba   Yeah straight towards us.

Jenny   Shit.

Ebba   And it keeps getting bigger and bigger . . . Suddenly, it's clear . . . That now something's terribly wrong. Everybody panics.

They start running and screaming. It's total chaos. Total chaos. The wall of snow is like fifty metres high and one hundred metres wide. And it's moving so fast. So, I grab

Vera and Harry and I try to pick them both up. But I can't.
So, I look for Tomas, to help carry the kids to safety . . .

And what I see is my husband grabbing his phone . . . and
running like hell away from us.

Beat.

Then everything goes white. I'm standing there with the
kids. There's this intensity and these sounds, like nothing
I've ever known. And I'm thinking that this is it. We're dead.
And I call out to Tomas . . . But he's not there.

Beat.

I don't know how long it all went on. And then . . . there is no
avalanche. That wall of snow closing in on us was only
avalanche smoke. The actual avalanche came to a stop before
reaching the restaurant. There I am, clutching my kids, and
suddenly the sky is blue again! Our lunch is still on the table.
Our drinks are still there. People start coming back and
realize that there was no bloody avalanche at all it was just a
false alarm. I don't know what to do, so I sit down and eat.

Beat.

And then Tomas comes back . . . And we don't *say anything*.
We just eat our lunch.

Beat.

So now I have a problem, right? Here I am in this fancy
resort, and I'm not happy. I'm not happy. It's not good, I
don't like it here, I want to go home.

Beat.

Tomas, say something! This is so fucking weird with you not
saying anything!

Silence.

Mats   When . . . When there's . . . In situations like these,
you're not always . . . aware of what you're doing. You just

try to survive it. You go into survival mode. And you know when you're in survival mode, you might not be able to live up to, you know, your regular values/ and moral code and all . . .

Ebba   Fine, but afterwards you need to own up to it. Admit what you did. That's fine. But you say you screwed up, you let everyone down and you apologise. You don't deny it happened.

Mats   But didn't . . .? What are your thoughts, Tomas?

Silence.

Ebba   Tomas, Mats is asking you a question, so could you please say something?

Tomas   Well –

Harry (*O/S*)   MUMMY! Mummy!

Tomas *looks to* **Ebba**.

Ebba   Ignore him ignore he'll fall asleep.

Harry (*O/S*)   Mummy!

Tomas   I can't ignore my kids.

Tomas *gets up and heads to* **Harry**'s *room*.

Ebba   What do I do?

Jenny   He was going to explain himself then. Maybe he's still processing it.

Silence.

Ebba   I'll go and check.

Mats   Yeah yeah sure of course.

Once **Ebba** *has gone* . . .

Mats   Jesus Christ . . .

Jenny   What the hell is going on?

Mats   I don't know I don't know. We came in. I was worried about my boner,/ now this.

Jenny   You've got to say something/ she was nearly *crying* there.

Mats   I'm not – What am I gonna say? Why are you such a bloody coward? This is their marriage, I'm not getting all up in their business, they're obviously *freaking out* about this,/ I have no intention of getting involved

Jenny   She is. He's not. He's just sat there not saying anything. I thought you said he was a great guy.

Mats   He is.

Jenny   He left his kids in a *fucking* – HEEYYY!

Ebba *returns.*

Mats   Heeyyy alright. Kids OK?

Ebba   All fine, I'm just going to take my wine.

Mats   The wine! Yes,/ the wine! Don't let it get warm.

Jenny   It is *so* good this wine.

Ebba *leaves.*

Jenny   What the hell is going on?

Mats   I don't know./ I didn't know a thing about this

Jenny   Why have you brought/ me into this?

Mats   I didn't – I didn't know – I didn't know this was going on. What can I do? Text ahead 'Hey Tomas, Still on for tonight? Just checking, you haven't left your kids in any avalanches, recently have you?/ Don't want to say the wrong thing.'

Jenny   They are not in a good place.

Mats   What am I meant to do?

Jenny   They are not in a good place. Their marriage.

Mats   So, should we leave? Should we go, or just stick around? We could leave a note/ I could write a note.

Jenny   We can't leave now otherwise it looks like we're judging.

Mats   OK, so we stay?

Jenny   But we can't stay,/ *they* need to talk about this.

Mats   So, what are you saying?/ We go stand on the balcony?

Jenny   They need to talk they need therapy.

Meanwhile in the kids' bedroom, **Tomas** *lies in bed with* **Harry** *and* **Ebba** *looks in, their exchange is hushed.*

Ebba   Is he OK?

Tomas   He's a bit upset. I'd better lie with him.

Ebba   Harry?

Tomas   Sh shh. He's nearly asleep.

Ebba *heads over and leans in.*

Ebba   He's fast asleep.

Tomas   I've only just got him off.

Ebba   He's sleeping.

Tomas   You're going to wake him.

Ebba   Come and talk Mats and Jenny are waiting.

Tomas   I'll be in, in a minute. You go.

Ebba   I'm not going without you.

Tomas   I've just got him off.

Ebba   Don't hide behind Harry.

Tomas   I am looking after my son.

It's a stand-off.

Eventually **Ebba** *re-joins* **Mats** *and* **Jenny** *in the room.*

Ebba   Sorry about this. Tomas. He wants to lie with Harry for a bit longer. I'm sorry. We've just struggled to talk about this, and I thought maybe with some friends/ we might be able to.

Jenny   It's fine it's fine.

Mats   This is why we're here.

Jenny *indicates for* **Mats** *to take the lead.*

Tomas *enters but lingers so he can eavesdrop, and no-one can see him.*

Mats   I think it could be good for you both to try and see all this in a wider context and in a more forgiving light.

Ebba   OK.

Mats   If you look at human beings and animals, the fact is, that when we're confronted by an extremely dangerous situation, it triggers survival mode. That forces you to react now! It's . . . It's a primitive force to just escape. We all have an idea of heroes or what heroes look like. And the pressure to be a hero and do heroic things in terrible situations. All the movies where the Dad stops at nothing to be reunited with his kids. But the truth is when reality is staring you in the face, and you're afraid you're going to die you know, very few of us are heroic.

Ebba   I didn't run.

Mats   Just look at the ferry in Estonia. Only 137 people survived and 850 people died on board. And these people . . . they trampled on dead bodies. They knocked down children and old people. They did terrible things, just to survive. Then they had to live with what they had done. But you can't punish them for those crimes. It's human. I get it.

Ebba   I can't identify with anyone who would trample on their own kids to survive.

Jenny   Me neither.

Mats   No . . . I mean what I mean is. I think./ What I mean is.

Ebba   That's not what this is about, not to me. My problem is that my natural instinct in that moment is for my children. It has to be. They're too little to fend for themselves. I'm their mother. It's my job. It's mine and Tomas' job to protect them. But his instinct was to run away.

Tomas *hangs his head in shame.*

Mats   But you need to consider everything Tomas is. Everything he's done for you; how much he loves you and the kids. He had a split-second reaction. If a drunk stormed in here and attacked you with a bottle, I'd punch him, even though I'm not a violent man I hate violence. But that's what I would do in that moment. But you don't really know what you would do. And maybe it would be different every time.

Ebba   I don't know. He's just . . . I don't know.

Tomas *enters.*

Tomas   It's . . . interesting when things like this happen. The differences. It shocked us, as a couple that we could have such different. That our perceptions of the situation could be so different. And I didn't realize that you saw it that way. You didn't tell me at the time. So, I carried on thinking we had the same take on things. Now I know we clearly don't.

Ebba   Then share your version with us Tomas?

Pause.

Everyone's waiting.

Tomas   But it's . . . It's not really relevant how I perceived it. Obviously for you, it was really dramatic. But for me . . .

Jenny *sits by* **Ebba** *to comfort her as she takes this blow.*

Mats   So you're not on board with the version Ebba just told us?

Tomas   No, I'm not. Not at all.

Mats   No?

Tomas   No. I really don't share her version of events. I don't. You are entitled to your own point of view Ebba. But I don't share it because it did, not, happen. It didn't happen and I'm sorry, but I won't be characterised this way in front of my friends, or the kids or anyone for that matter. At some point I have to stand up for myself and defend my character. What you are saying, categorically, did, not, happen.

Tomas *takes a drink.*

Mats   OK, well that makes it all/ a bit more

Ebba   We've got it all on film.

Beat.

It's on your phone. Let's just watch it. See who's telling the truth. Would you like to see it?

Jenny *and* **Mats** *nod.*

Jenny   Ye/ ah.

Mats   Ye/ ah.

Jenny   Ab/ solutely.

Mats   Let's take/ a look yeah.

Tomas   I think we've had enough of this.

Ebba   No.

Tomas   I really . . . don't see what this/ is going to achieve at this point.

Ebba   I'll go get your phone.

Ebba *leaves to fetch* **Tomas'** *phone.*

Long silence.

Tomas   Obviously, it *was* scary . . . / I'm not saying it wasn't scary.

Mats   Yeah, yeah of course./ I understand.

Ebba *arrives with the phone.*

Tomas   But we're all here. Harry and Vera are OK and at the end of the/ day, that's what's.

Ebba   What's your pin code?

Tomas   That's what's important.

Ebba   What's your pin code?

Tomas   This is a bit much Ebba./ Can we just

Ebba   I'd like you to see this. To finish this . . . I really/ need to do this. All right?

Tomas   It might upset you again. It might upset everyone this was a/ very triggering

Ebba   Pin code? Pin code.

Tomas   My birthday.

Ebba *punches in his pin code.*

Tomas   OK. Go ahead go ahead.

Ebba   Good. Are you all going to look . . .?

Mats and **Jenny** *scrabble around* **Ebba**. *The video plays and* **Tomas** *watches them watching his phone.*

Ebba: Here . . . Here it comes . . . That's us at the table . . .

Harry and **Vera**'s *screams can be heard on the video.*

Ebba   You're filming, right? You can see he's filming because we're all in shot. And then . . . here he runs away.

Beat.

You can clearly see someone running away here with the camera.

Beat.

And I think.

Ebba *winds the video back.*

Yep. That's him screaming.

Ebba *winds the video back.*

Yeah. That's definitely him screaming.

Ebba *winds the video back.*

Running. And screaming.

She winds the video again.

Running and screaming away from us, as the avalanche comes.

Beat.

Do you agree *now* that you ran away from the table?

Tomas   I agree, that it looks like, I'm running.

Ebba   It looks like you're running because you *were* running. Weren't you?

Silence.

Mats   Tomas maybe, maybe you were thinking . . . In an avalanche situation, it's pretty tricky to get out from under the snow . . . So maybe you planned to go back and dig them out?

Just like when cabin pressure drops in an aeroplane, they say that parents should put their masks on first before you put one on their kids. It feels counter-intuitive to protect yourself first. But maybe that's what you had in your mind So you actually did the right thing for a situation like this.

Beat.

That was what you were thinking, right? Wasn't it? When you were running.

Ebba   And screaming. Running and screaming.

Lights down.

Scene Thirteen

Hotel Corridor

Ebba   Thanks for coming.

Mats   Thanks for a great/ night!

Jenny   Great/ night!

Ebba   Sorry if it was a bit . . .

Mats   No!

Jenny   No it was great!

Ebba   OK. See you tomorrow.

Ebba *goes.*

Mats   Holy shit . . .

Jenny   OhmyGod. What the hell?

Mats   I know right.

Jenny   What was *that*?

Mats   I know. Oh My God.

Jenny   Poor Ebba.

Mats   Well, yeah.

Jenny   She's completely torn up by it.

Mats   Yeah.

Beat.

And Tomas too.

Jenny   Well.

Mats   The both of them. It's really sad.

Jenny   It is really sad.

Mats   I know.

Jenny   I feel so sorry for her. Did you see her face?

Mats   Mm . . . So sad.

Jenny   I mean I wonder how I would react if you did that to me?

Mats   Pff . . . Right.

Jenny   You might have run too, left your kids behind. You don't know. No one can be sure of anything like that.

Mats   Well, you might have run as well.

Jenny   But we're talking about you and Tomas.

Mats   Why?/ Don't put me in the. . .

They silence themselves as:

A young **Man** *stripped to the waist with sunglasses and antlers on, walks between them.*

Antler **Man** *offers* **Mats** *a fist bump and* **Mats** *finds himself fist bumping.*

Jenny   I think I would react just like Ebba. I wouldn't be able to run.

Mats   And I would?

Jenny   I think you could yeah.

Mats   Whoa whoa whoa what are you saying here what are we saying here?

Mats *refuses to get in the lift.*

Jenny   (*laughing*)   Don't get upset. I'm just . . .

Mats   What am I meant to do with that?/ Just casually . . .

Jenny   Don't make this about you.

Mats   Of course it's about me, you just said that I'd leave you and the kids in the avalanche.

Jenny   We don't have kids.

Mats   I do.

Beat.

You're having a go at me, for something Tomas has done.

Mats *puts his hand on the lift to stop it closing.*

Jenny   I'm just saying. You're more capable of running away than I am.

Mats   Why?

Jenny   Because you're a man and I'm a woman.

Silence.

Mats   So this isn't about me per se. It's about men/ and women.

Jenny   I don't know I haven't thought about it until tonight/ and all that in there.

Mats   It's about men and women. And you think there's a difference. All men are like this. And all women are like that./ That's interesting. That's very interesting.

Jenny   No . . . I mean . . . I'm not . . . Well,/ like this . . . what I mean is.

Mats   No it's really interesting. That you're happy to generalise about an entire *gender*!

The **Cleaner** *walks past, really slowly.*

Mats   Good night.

Jenny   Good night.

They wait.

And wait.

And wait – maybe the **Cleaner** *empties a bin.*

Jenny *and* **Mats** *stand in agonising silence until he eventually leaves.*

Jenny   What I mean is. I don't mean all men and women are like one way or another you can't generalise like that about people.

Mats   Thank you. We can agree on that.

Mats *offers a hand to shake.*

Jenny   But you and Tomas are the same kind of man.

Mats *drops the hand.*

Mats   What does that mean? We're skiing buddies. Couple of days hanging out once a year doesn't mean we're the same person.

Jenny   I know. I'm not . . .

Mats   I don't even know/ what car he drives.

Jenny   I'm not saying that. I'm just saying . . . Like. You're both made of the same ideas. I don't know, if you compare the two of you with, say, Filip . . . Filip would *never* run away, *never* abandon/ his family like that. Never.

Mats   What? Filip, who is *twenty-one* and still living with his parents, and who *doesn't* have any kids, he would defend his family, but I, an actual father wouldn't?

Jenny   Hypothetically speaking yes. (*Off* **Mats**.) There's a huge difference between your generation and ours! That's what I'm trying to say. Like there's a big difference between you and your father./ You take on more responsibility for your kids than his generation did.

Mats   So, so hypothetically, you think it's more probable that Filip, a skinny little app designer, would protect his family rather than me because I was born in the seventies?

Jenny *thinks this is a fair assessment.*

Mats   I have *always* taken care of my family. I have *always* made sure that they were very well taken care of. OK? I take care of my kids.

Jenny   So, where are they now?

Mats   You know that.

Jenny   And your ex-wife?

Mats   In Oslo.

Beat.

What?

Jenny   You say you do everything for them, but *she's* taking care of them right now. *You're* taking a twenty-three-year-old girl on vacation who you've been dating for six months.

Mats   Is that a problem?

Jenny   Not for me. But what do you think your ex-wife thinks?

Jenny *steps into the lift.*

Mats *really doesn't want to join her.*

Eventually he does.

The lift door closes.

Scene Fourteen

Hotel Room

Ebba *clears up the detritus around the room.*

Tomas *sits in the same position he was when he watched the video.*

Ebba *passes carrying some things.*

Tomas   Ebba.

Long, painful silence.

Is there any more wine?

Ebba   I'll check.

Tomas   Thanks, you.

Tomas *sits in silence.*

He turns his phone over, so the screen is no longer tormenting him.

Ebba *brings a half full bottle back and places it on the table.*

She starts to wipe down the table. **Tomas** *lifts his glass, and then the bottle.*

Tomas   Oh hang on.

Ebba   Thanks.

Tomas   No problem.

Tomas *watches* **Ebba** *wiping down. Eventually she finishes and heads to the bedroom.*

Tomas   Are you sleeping in there?

Ebba   Yes.

Tomas   I'll stay here then.

Ebba (*back turned*)   Great.

Tomas   Great. Great. Great! Great. Just great.

Tomas *pours himself a glass of wine.*

Ebba   What?

Tomas   Shall we talk about what just happened?

Ebba   I'm not making a scene that will upset the kids.

Tomas   No of course because you never upset the kids it's only me who upsets the kids.

Ebba   Shut up Tomas you pathetic man.

Silence.

I have had it! Doing all the work for the both of us. Doing all the work so that there's a family here for you when you can be bothered to turn up. And when you do turn up, you abandon us and lie, I've had it. I deserve more. The kids deserve more.

Tomas   OK, I made a mistake. A big mistake . . .

Ebba   I'm not talking about the avalanche. That was just the thing that opened everyone's eyes to you.

Tomas   Ebba, I'm sorry. I was embarrassed/ . . . but don't

Ebba   I don't want to talk about it. I don't. I don't want to talk to you. I just want to get through the rest of this and see where we are when we get home. I'm not doing it here.

Tomas   What do you mean 'see where we are'?

Ebba   I mean, see where we are.

Tomas   As a couple?

Ebba   Yes. We'll see where we are when we get home.

Tomas   I'm scared now.

Ebba   So am I.

Pause.

Tomas   Well. What are we talking/ about?

Ebba   I'm not doing this here! I'm not.

Tomas But you're scaring me! I want to sort this out. We need to sort this out.

Ebba We'll talk about this when we get home.

Tomas Are you leaving me?

Lights down

Interval.

Scene Fifteen

Mats and Jenny's Room

Darkness.

Jenny *reaches out and turns on a bedside light to reveal:*

Mats *sat up in bed – wide awake staring into the darkness.*

Jenny What's the matter?

Mats Nothing.

Jenny Can you not sleep?

Mats Go back to sleep.

Jenny *tries.*

She can't. She rolls over to **Mats** *and cuddles up to him.*

Jenny Come on. Go to sleep.

Beat.

Mats I just . . . I'm just trying to figure out what I have said or done to make you think I would abandon you and our children in that situation.

Jenny Hmm?

Mats What have I done? I can't think of anything.

Jenny Is this. Is this about Tomas?

Mats   No, it's about *me*. What have I said or done that would make you think I was capable of that?

Jenny   Nothing. You haven't said anything. Go to sleep.

Sensing **Mats** *is not moving. She turns back to him and sees he is deeply worried – she's hurt him. She adopts a more conciliatory and subservient approach and sits up.*

Jenny   Listen, you haven't said or done anything. It was just hypothetical.

Beat.

I know that you would do anything to protect your family, I really do. And I really believe you would try to protect me if anything happened.

Mats   I thought, one of the things you liked about me, was that you felt safe.

Jenny   I do.

Mats   But . . . you said Tomas and me are the same kind of men. You had suspicions about me earlier.

Jenny   I didn't. It was just . . . a bit crazy trying to understand it all that's all. But I know you'd look after me.

Mats   Do you?

Jenny   Yes, absolutely.

Mats   Really?

Jenny   Yes. Now go to sleep.

Mats   Are you just saying this so you can go to sleep?

Jenny   No, I mean it. I do.

Mats *looks at her, trying to see the truth.*

Jenny   Are you OK now?

Mats   Yeah, I'm just being silly.

Lights down.

Lights up.

Time has passed – **Mats** *is pacing.* **Jenny** *is sat on the bed with her head in her hands.*

Mats You said don't think about it. Why not think about it? Why not think about it? Do you mean; don't think about it because there's something about me/ neither of us want to address? Some deep-seated cowardice at the depths of my soul.

Jenny Pleaaaase.

Mats Something horrible. Don't think about it you said. Maybe you said that because if I think about it *too* much, I might discover something about myself that confirms what you suspect of me? Maybe that's why you said that. Is that why you said it?

Jenny No. I promise. Let's put an end to this. Please come back to bed.

Lights down.

Lights up.

More time has passed – **Jenny** *is sat on the floor.*

Mats *is stripped to the waist pouring whisky from a bottle into his mouth.*

Mats Filip! Filip for fuck's sake!

Beat.

Fucking *Filip*. He can't even drive *the twat*. He'll save you, yeah, he'll fucking save you, as long as it's *walking distance* or on a bus route. 'Don't worry kids! Don't worry! Filip is coming, he's coming to save us on his stupid long skateboard covered in *stickers*.'

Jenny   I'm guessing you're drunk and tired and now
you're stuck in some mood,/ I don't know what it is, and I
don't know what I can say.

Mats   Here he comes! Watch his skinny white legs push his
skateboard up this mountain we're trapped on.

Jenny   You're boring now.

Mats   Oh, am I? Am I really? I'm sorry. What if I? What if I
said to you, if I said to you, you're the kind of woman; 'Lots
of women can't have kids and I think you're one of them.'
'You are the kind of woman who can't have kids.' 'I don't
think you're female enough for that. But Merle. Now Merle,
looks like a fertile heifer. She looks like the kind of woman,
who could bear me a whole football team of fat babies.'

Jenny   Then I'd say, 'That's too bad!' And then I'd go to
bed because you need to go to bed. OK? It's over.

Bedside lamps off.

Lights down.

Bedside lamps on.

Jenny *is curled up in a chair. Mess is strewn all over the floor.*

Mats *has his ski goggles on and long-johns on his head. He is
waving a ski pole around as he speaks.*

Mats   AND I CRACKED HIM ON THE HEAD LIKE
THIS! AND THEN ANOTHER LIKE THAT! AND I FELT
POWERFUL. AND I TURNED TO MY MOTHER WHO
WAS COVERED IN VOMIT AND I SAID: are you sleeping?

Jenny *startles.*

Jenny   No. No./ I was checking the phone . . .

Mats   You were sleeping, how could you?/ How could you?

Jenny   I promise I wasn't. I'm listening,/ I'm listening with
my eyes closed.

Mats I'm pouring my heart out here, this is powerful stuff. This is a special time. I'm really getting into some stuff here. Why?

He straightens a legging from his head.

Mats Why won't you take me seriously?

Jenny I have to go to bed now.

Mats FUCK THE BED!

He throws his ski pole on the floor!

Mats STOP GOING ON ABOUT THE FUCKING BED! YOU AND THE – RIGHT! I'LL SHOW YOU THE FUCKING BED.

Mats *runs to the side of the bed and bends down to lift it up and toss it over.*

But it's really heavy.

Mats *strains.*

Mats YAAAAAAAAAAHHHHHWHYSITSOHEAVY! I can't. I can't it's YAAAAAAHHHHHAAAITSATTACHED. It's attached to something. I can't, drilled to the floor.

Mats *collapses on the bed in exhaustion. He then throws all the pillows and sheets off and pulls off the bottom sheet and wraps it up into a ball and throws it.*

He manages to push the mattress a bit off the bed.

He stands atop the bed as champion – having defeated his enemy.

Mats *Now* will you listen to me?

Jenny I don't think there's anything on your mind that you haven't already said. You're going over and over and over/ the same thing.

Mats Oh this is trivial is it? My feelings, my PAIN is trivial. You can't talk to me like that I was a fat child/ this is all just some big

Jenny   No. I upset you and that's important. And I want us to be good. But I also don't want to miss a day's skiing tomorrow. The mountain. We've come here for.

Beat.

Skiing? You love this mountain. You brought me here to ski. Not fight. And if you want to ski. Then. You need to sleep. Come on. Look at you. You're exhausted.

Mats   I am pretty tired. Being in tune with your emotions, it's actually quite, actually quite draining you know?

Jenny   Yeah I know.

Jenny *picks up the discarded bedsheet, but he points a ski pole at her.*

Mats   Stop. I need to know that you trust me. It's very important to me.

Jenny   I trust you. OK?

Mats   Why are you smiling like that? What? Is this a joke?/ My feelings are a laughing matter?

Jenny   I can't take this seriously anymore. We've been going around in circles for hours! I trust you, OK? I trust you. I trust you.

He tries to see if she's hiding something. He can't see it. She seems sincere.

Jenny   Now. Could we *please* get some sleep?

Mats   OK . . .

Together they put the bed back together.

Mats   That was intense. I really worked through some stuff there, I feel, I feel great actually.

Jenny   Good I'm glad.

Mats   I felt like I was really accessing *me*.

Jenny   Great. I'm glad.

The bed is re-made, **Jenny** *climbs in immediately.*

Mats   Feel like I understand myself better now.

Jenny   Goooood. Now. Go to sleep.

Jenny *turns the bedside light off.*

Darkness.

Jenny (*relieved*)   Ah . . .

Mats (*relieved*)   And now, to sleep.

Jenny   Thank God! No wonder your wife wanted a divorce.

Bedside light on.

Mats *stares at her.*

Scene Sixteen

Hotel Bathroom/Fantasy Sequence/Mountain

Movement sequence: **Tomas** *stands perfectly still, as* **Ebba**, **Vera** *and* **Harry** *brush their teeth, wash their faces, spray deodorant, brush hair. But now the taps are replaced by Gazex tubes that boom and flash as the family get dressed.*

BOOM! **Ebba**, **Vera** *and* **Harry** *take cover and* **Ebba** *protects the kids. They carry on brushing their teeth and washing their faces and then BOOM!* **Ebba**, **Vera** *and* **Harry** *take cover and* **Ebba** *protects them. They carry on their morning routines and BOOM! They take cover and* **Ebba** *protects them.* **Tomas** *watches how the family run to each other and he's outside the safety of them. He turns a tap on and steam rises like avalanche smoke . . .*

Tomas *is alone, in his ski gear, on the mountain.*

At his feet **Ebba** *is on her knees, crying and digging in the snow. She is distressed, searching for the buried children – she finds gloves/ boots sticking out.*

Tomas *stares at her – this is what is haunting him now.*

Mats *arrives, and* **Tomas** *snaps out of his daydream nighmare.*

Mats   Um . . . Done uh, done much before now?

Tomas   Huh?

Mats   Skiing. Done much.

Tomas   No. A bit. Mainly with. Family.

Mats   Cut loose today then?

Tomas   Yeah.

Mats   Great.

Tomas   Yeah.

Mats   OK.

Tomas   OK.

Mats   Um? Fancy skiing off piste today? Get away from. Everything.

Tomas   Absolutely! Yeah. That would be yeah, let's get away from the . . . crowds.

Mats   Yeah. Let's go. Let's go higher up.

Tomas   Yeah. Let's go. Up there. Higher.

Mats   Get to the top. Trek for a bit. Fancy that?

Tomas *stares at where* **Ebba** *was.*

Tomas   I do yeah. Yeah.

Mats   Cool.

Tomas   It's so bright.

Mats   Put your goggles on.

Movement sequence as **Mats** *and* **Tomas** *skilfully ski together down the slope.*

Mats   So what shall we go for? We could try the couloir. It's on the right when you're at the peak. Or. I can't see anyone else. Maybe try the other side? We've got the whole mountain to ourselves pretty much, just need to choose the route. Other side looks quiet.

Tomas   I'm. I'm not sure I want to ski anymore.

Mats   What? Are you OK?

Tomas   Yeah. No.

Mats   Do you want a drink?

Tomas   No.

Mats   You want to head home?

Tomas   No.

Beat.

Tomas   Can we just, talk instead?

Mats *nearly falls down the mountain with disappointment.*

Mats   Yeah. Sure. We can talk.

Long, painful silence.

What shall we talk about?

Tomas   I'm not sure.

Long, painful silence.

Mats   So beautiful up here.

Long, painful silence.

Something you want to talk about?

Long, painful silence.

Tomas   I don't know.

Long, painful silence.

Mats   You feeling all right?

Long, painful silence.

Tomas   I don't know.

Mats   Maybe you should try screaming?

Tomas   Huh?

Mats   Screaming. Seriously. I spent two years in therapy and it didn't do a bloody thing. Then one night I just screamed into a pillow for five minutes solid and felt a hell of a lot better. It's physical, something is stuck in your body and you have to get it out. I mean it. Nobody can hear you, so go for it! It's just me.

Tomas   Screaming?

Mats   Yeah.

Tomas   Like a child?

Mats   Yeah like a child.

Tomas   I'm supposed to sit here and scream.

Mats   On the count of three.

Tomas   No,/ no way.

Mats   On the count of three.

Tomas   No.

Mats   One,/ two

Tomas   I am not doing it absolutely no

Mats   Three.

HHHAHHHHHAHHHHHHHHHHHAHHHHHH

Tomas *screams.*

Mats   Good. Now you need to really scream like you mean it.

Beat.

From the depths of your belly.

Tomas No forget it, it's stupid. I feel stupid.

Mats Come on! One, two,

Tomas No no, forget it I don't want.

Mats three. . .

Tomas AAAHAHHHHHHAAAA/
AAAAAAAAHAHHHHAAAAAHHHHHH

Mats Yes. Do it for real! TOMAS! FUCKING HELL.
AGAIN!

Tomas *screams again – louder, more primal more desperate.*

Tomas AAAHHHHHHAAAAAAHHHHHHHAAAHHH/
AAAAAHHHHHH Damn it!!! Fucking hell! PISS
BOLLOCKS FUCK WANK SHIT! CUNTING FUCK.
HELL. BOLLOCKS.

Mats Good!

Tomas *falls back in the snow.*

Mats Better.

Beat.

I feel better and I'm just standing here. Better?

Tomas I think so.

Mats It's a weight lifted off. The mind and body. It's all one
thing. You literally can't fix anything these days without
screaming everyone knows that. There's whole books
written about it. You did some good work on yourself there.

Tomas You think?

Mats Definitely. And the swearing. That's got to be good
right?

Tomas Yeah.

Mats Yeah right.

Tomas   So, what now? Do we. Do we talk now?

Long silence.

Mats   Yeah. Or you could scream again?

Tomas   Think I'm done screaming.

Long silence.

Mats   Then we should probably get pissed.

Lights down.

Scene Seventeen

Slope-side bar

Tomas *and* **Mats** *relax with a beer in deck chairs. Party people mill around, drinking, dancing and socialising.*

Mats   He's just hanging around her all the time, if I go to the bar, or to the toilet, or turn around for a second he appears and is all over her, he's in love with her but she doesn't see it.

Tomas   She doesn't see it.

Mats   No!/ It's so obvious . . .

A **Female Skier** *approaches.*

Female Skier   Hi guys. Are you having fun?

Tomas   Huh?

Female Skier   Are you having fun?

Tomas   Yes, great day thanks. We've been/ skiing off –

Female Skier   I came to tell you that my friend is standing over there . . .

Tomas   Yeah?

Female Skier   She thinks that you're the best-looking man in the bar.

The men laugh it off.

Tomas   OK. Thank you.

Female Skier   You're welcome. Have a good night.

Tomas   You too.

*The **Female Skier** leaves.*

Tomas *revels in the news.*

Mats *and* **Tomas** *cheers.*

Tomas   Still got it.

Mats   Still got it.

Tomas   Class is permanent.

Mats   Form is temporary.

Tomas   Amen to that. You remember that time in that bar that used to be/ called Lux or something and that girl came in and she –?

*The **Female Skier** returns.*

Female Skier   Hi.

Tomas (*familiar*)   Oh hi again.

Female Skier   Sorry. I had to come back again. I made a mistake. She didn't, she didn't mean you. She meant someone else.

Tomas   Huh?

Female Skier   My friend. She didn't mean you. I got it wrong, she meant someone else. Sorry. It was my fault.

Tomas   OK. Fine. Thank you.

Female Skier   She pointed, and I thought she meant you. But she didn't.

Tomas   Oh right.

Female Skier   I'm sorry.

Tomas   It's fine.

Female Skier   The guy she meant is right behind you so.

Tomas   OK.

Female Skier   It's my fault.

Tomas   Fine.

Female Skier   I thought I should tell you.

Tomas   Why?

Pause.

Female Skier   Because. You're not the guy she liked.

Tomas   Why not just let me think she meant me?

Female Skier   Because I made a mistake, she meant that guy.

Tomas   I know but –

Female Skier   She didn't mean you.

Mats   It would have been kinder to just let the mistake stand uncorrected/ and let Tomas

Female Skier   She doesn't find you attractive and you might try something later.

Tomas   I'm married so.

Female Skier   Where is she then?

Tomas   I'm just sitting here having a drink! I didn't ask for people to come up to me and tell me they don't find me attractive. Who wants that to happen?

Mats   I don't. It's never happened to me,/ but still.

Female Skier   I don't want it to be awkward for her, she wants to have a good time, she doesn't want you to come on to her later thinking she'd given you a green light.

Tomas   She asked you to come over here again?

Female Skier   Yes, she really doesn't want you to buy her a drink or.

Tomas   OK.

Female Skier   Ask for her number or.

Tomas   OK.

Female Skier   Try and talk to her or anything like that.

Tomas   OK fine. Loud and clear. Thank you.

Female Skier   Or look at her.

Tomas *can just about manage a hard stare.*

Female Skier   She just pointed and . . . OK.

Tomas   OK.

Female Skier *walks off and approaches the attractive* **Male Skier** *behind* **Tomas** *to deliver the compliment to the right man.*

Tomas   What the hell?

Mats   Would we have ever done that/ when we were their age?

Tomas   I'm just sitting here. I haven't done *anything* and I get all this. Is she taking the piss?

Mats   She's taking the piss.

Tomas   She's taking the piss.

Mats   She thinks we're mugs.

Tomas   We are mugs if we take that.

Mats (*to the women*)   Are you taking the piss?

Female Skier   No, no, no.

Tomas   You think we're funny?

Female Skier   No I wasn't it/ was just my friend pointed.

Tomas   You and your friends want to laugh at us? At me. You're taking the piss out of me, what because I'm old?

Tomas *stands to confront the women.*

Mats   Take it easy.

The attractive **Male Skier** *interrupts to diffuse the situation.*

Male Skier   Whoa whoa whoa! Calm down. Relax. Chill.

Tomas   They're taking the piss. I'm just sitting here having a drink minding my own business and she comes over and says I'm not even allowed to look at a girl.

Male Skier   Are you staring at her?

Tomas   She came onto me first for Christ's sake.

Male Skier   You need to chill out, I'm not gonna tell you again.

Tomas   Stop telling me to chill out alright.

Male Skier   Step back now or you and me are gonna have a problem.

Tomas   We already have a problem *Pierre*; your friends are taking the piss.

Male Skier   You want a problem with me we can take it/ outside.

Mats   There's no problem there's no problem. Tomas.

Male Skier   Have we got a problem?/ We can sort it out now.

Mats   There's no problem. Tomas. There's no problem. Tomas . . . Tomas.

Tomas   OK.

Male Skier   We're cool?

Pause.

Mats   We're cool. Tomas.

Tomas   Yeah.

Male Skier   Great, well why don't you sit down? Drink your beer relax and everything will be nice.

Mats   Tomas, come on, come sit down.

Male Skier   Relax. Take a seat.

Tomas   I'll take my seat when I want to take my seat, you go back over there and take your seat and I'll take my seat at a time of my choosing.

Tomas *makes a big show of taking his time. Maybe stretching a little, while everyone watches waiting for the situation to be defused.* **Tomas** *goes to sit, and then changes his mind, and the dusts the seat down, and then thinks about sitting down. And eventually after a final stretch sits down.*

And everyone, finally, returns to their seats.

Mats *and* **Tomas** *share a look.*

Mats   'At a time of my choosing.'

Mats *and* **Tomas** *laugh.*

Scene Eighteen

Hotel Corridor

A tired, and possibly a bit drunk, **Tomas** *is at the door of the family room.*

He checks all of his pockets. He can't find a key.

Tomas   Ebba? Open up! It's me. I'm back. Can't find my – can you open up? Your phone's died. Are you in there? Can you let me in? Would be really great to talk. Hope this isn't some kind of punishment. That would be . . . that would be. Not cool.

The **Cleaner** *walks past.*

Tomas   Ah! Excuse moi! Jai uh, perdu uh, key card. Ma femme has the other one and uh, elle este uh, sortie.

The **Cleaner** *takes a card and presses it against a sensor which buzzes and negative sound.*

Tomas   Thank you.

He tries again – still buzzes negative.

The **Cleaner** *is confused. He tries again.*

Tomas   Something wrong?

Beat.

You're trying too quick-trop uh rapide trop rapide. This is your hotel!

Tomas *takes the card and tries – it doesn't work.*

Tomas   EBBA! ARE YOU IN THERE? Elle est sortie. EBBA! EBBA! She's not in there.

Tomas *is left staring at the* **Cleaner**.

Tomas   I'll try l'accueil merci.

The **Cleaner** *shrugs his shoulders and takes his card and walks on.*

Tomas *is left outside the door.*

Tomas   EBBA!

Lights down.

Scene Nineteen

Hotel Lobby

Exhausted **Tomas** *enters the hotel foyer.*

Receptionist   Bonsoir monsieur.

Tomas   Bonsoir, je'need un nouveau key card merci?

Receptionist   Oui pas de problème, what is your room number?

Tomas   247.

Receptionist   D'accord, are your key cards lost or in your room?

Tomas   Lost.

Receptionist   D'accord – I will have to programme two new keys.

Tomas   That's no problem I'll stay in the room until they get back.

Receptionist   Do you know where your wife is?

Tomas   Obviously not, because if I did, I'd just go and find them.

Receptionist   It's just, if I disable your old keys to activate new ones and your family are in the pool, or the sauna, or the spa area, or the games room, their card it no longer works. They might not be able to get out or open their lockers.

Tomas   What? That's ridiculous.

Receptionist   Can you call her?

Tomas   My phone has died can you charge my phone?

Receptionist   Désolé Monsieur. We're not allowed to charge phones here I'm sorry.

Tomas   Do you have a charger I can borrow then?

Receptionist   We're not allowed to lend chargers to guests.

Tomas   Why not?

Receptionist   They steal them.

Tomas   So what am I supposed to do?

A magnificently French shrug.

Receptionist   You could pay extra for a third key.

Tomas   Fine give me an extra key.

Receptionist   There is a charge.

Tomas   Fine whatever.

Receptionist   Alors. Cent dix, that'll be one hundred and ten Euro. Would you like to pay by card?

Tomas   A hundred and ten Euros? It's a piece of plastic.

Receptionist   Je sais monsieur. It is company policy.

Tomas   I'm not paying a hundred and ten Euros.

Receptionist   Désolé monsieur this is company policy.

Tomas   And this has never happened before?

Receptionist   Oui, this is why we give two keys. One key and one spare.

Tomas   And you've never had families doing different things and someone loses a key? No-one loses anything and everyone does everything together? All the time? This is the resort where everyone's just perfect? 'We don't need another key we're perfect? We never lose anything and besides we're always together!' No-one ever argues, no-one ever needs any space, no-one ever needs to go up onto the mountain and scream into the abyss because of what their life has become?

Receptionist   I'm on eight Euros an hour.

Tomas   Which way's the sauna?

Tomas *puts his gloves back on and heads out.*

Scene Twenty

The Mountain

Movement sequence as **Tomas** *trudges around going from building to building – everywhere he looks there are happy families!*

Gazex tubes boom throughout this sequence as **Tomas** *falls into a happy-family nightmare!*

Tomas   ALLEZ!

Happy couples! Kissing couples!

Tomas   LASSIE MOI UHH PASSER!

Tomas *is buffeted back and forth by the happy families.*

Tomas   GET OUT OF MY BLOODY WAY!

Even the **Cleaner** *walks past with his arms around someone!*

Tomas *falls and he is face to face . . . with a Gazex tube!*

Tomas   AAAHHHHHHA!!!

He gets up and runs and is swept along with . . . A HUGE crowd of drunk, stripped-to-the-waist stag-doers charging the stage, screaming and shouting with the **Man** *stripped to the waist wearing sunglasses and antlers from earlier. They swamp* **Tomas** *(maybe they pick him up and carry him?) past a sign saying 'Sauna'.*

Scene Twenty-One

Sauna

The macho party of drunk stag-doers are now tightly packed like sardines in a steaming sauna with **Tomas** *in the middle and they SCREAM, SCREAM and SCREAM. Some of them hold Gazex tubes aloft as trophies they have broken and stolen!*

And then the lights come up and they stop screaming – **Tomas** *is bemused he looks around – baffled.*

Lights go down – SCREAM! SCREAM! SCREAM! – **Tomas**
startles!

Lights come up and they stop – **Tomas** *looks around – why are they
doing this?*

Lights go down – SCREAM! SCREAM! SCREAM!

Tomas *SCREAMS!*

Scene Twenty-Two

Hotel Corridor

Ebba (*on phone*)   Yes, I'll check what time we land. I was
thinking . . . would it be OK, if I came to stay with you for a
few days. Everything's fine, I just need a few days . . .

A harassed **Tomas** *arrives from the other end.*

Tomas   Where have you been?

Ebba   Oh Tomas is here.

Tomas   I've been searching for you all over!

Tomas   Who's that?

Ebba   It's Mum. Everything's fine, the dog's fine. The kids
are in there.

Ebba *indicates for* **Tomas** *to head into the room.*

Tomas *doesn't.*

Ebba *indicates again.*

Tomas *waits, encroaching on her privacy.* **Ebba** *steps away
from him.*

She loses her nerve.

Ebba (*on the phone, changing tack*)   Yeah. So thanks for that.
Yeah everything's fine I'd better go. Yes OK, love you.
Love you.

Tomas *goes to* **Ebba** *and tries to hug her but* **Ebba** *moves away quickly.*

Ebba   Bye OK, bye.

Tomas *manages to get his arm around* **Ebba**.

Ebba   Stop it.

Tomas   Stop what?

Ebba   Stop this! All of it! You.

Tomas   Me?

Ebba   Yes you.

Tomas   What does that mean?

Beat.

WHAT DOES THAT MEAN?

Ebba   You know what I mean.

Harry *and* **Vera** *appear in the corridor.*

Ebba   It's OK/ kids.

Vera   Mum?/ Is he?

Ebba   It's OK/ go back into the room.

Vera   Are you, OK?

Ebba   Yes./ I'm fine.

Tomas   She's fine.

Vera   Why is he shouting/ at you?

Tomas   I wasn't shouting.

Vera   You were.

Tomas   I raised/ my (voice)

Harry   You sounded/ angry.

Tomas   Go back/ inside please.

Vera   What's he angry about?

Tomas   I wasn't/ angry.

Ebba   Daddy's angry with himself and he thinks he can take it out on me.

Everyone looks to **Tomas**.

Tomas   Well . . . Look can I talk to Mummy/ in private please?

Harry   No you can't shout at her.

Tomas   I'm not/ going to. I promise.

Harry   No you're gonna shout at her again.

Tomas   Just let me . . . let me talk to her.

Vera   No we're not going anywhere.

Harry   We're not leaving her.

Vera *and* **Harry** *go to* **Ebba**.

Tomas   Come on I'm not going to do anything! OK, I'm sorry. I'm sorry. I raised my voice. Ebba here you are. I'm sorry. Forgive me everyone forgive me now can I just please, have a conversation with my wife, in privacy. Thank you. Just give us some privacy.

Harry   No!

Tomas   I'm not asking you I'm telling you, leave us alone.

Vera   We're not leaving you alone with Mum.

Tomas   GET IN THE ROOM.

Ebba   Don't shout at them.

Vera   We're not going in the room!

Tomas   WHY NOT?

Vera   BECAUSE WE DON'T TRUST YOU.

Tomas's *shoulders sink.*

He looks to **Ebba** *and to the kids.*

Defeated, he walks further down the corridor and then slumps down against a wall.

Long pause.

Ebba   Kids, actually let me talk to Daddy alone, we need to talk about some grown-up things in private OK? It's OK. I'm OK. I'll be in, in a minute. OK? In you go. In you go.

Beat.

I'll be fine. I promise. In you go. I just need to speak to Daddy.

Vera   Are you sure?

Ebba   I'm sure. In you go.

Harry   We'll be listening.

Ebba   Go and look at your iPad.

Vera   Don't be shouting, it's embarrassing.

Ebba   We won't shout I promise.

Harry *and* **Vera** *head back into the room.* **Ebba** *turns to* **Tomas** *who has slumped on the floor with his head in his hands, crying.*

Ebba *watches* **Tomas** *for a while.*

Ebba *approaches* **Tomas** *who is crying into his hands.*

Ebba   You're just pretending.

Tomas   What?

Ebba   You're not crying for real. Hello? You're not crying.

Tomas *shows his face.*

Tomas   OK, maybe I'm not.

Ebba *walks away.*

Tomas   But what should I do? I'm trying to get some sympathy here. I'm trying to communicate here with you I'm trying to be honest.

Ebba   Then try! For once in your life try Tomas.

Tomas *searches for the words but they don't come.* **Ebba** *turns to walk away.*

Tomas   Ebba, Ebba . . . Come here. Ebba!

Ebba   No.

Tomas   Ebba please! OK. OK I'll try I'll try.

Ebba *stops.*

Tonas   I get it.

Ebba   Get what?

Tomas   That . . . you're . . . I get it.

Ebba   Get *what* Tomas?

Tomas   I get, that you're disappointed in the person I've become.

Beat.

You don't have to say it. I see it in your eyes. I hear it in your voice. The way you are with me. I get it.

Beat.

You're disappointed.

Ebba   Stop making it my fault. This is not what the problem is.

Tomas   OK! I'm disappointed! I'm disappointed.

Beat.

In who I am.

Beat.

The person I've become.

Beat.

That person . . . If I think of him as another person then . . .

Beat.

I can say.

Beat.

I, hate him. I do, I hate him. And.

Beat.

I can't, forgive him.

Beat.

In fact I don't want to forgive him because he doesn't deserve it.

Beat.

He doesn't. So I don't really know what to do.

Ebba   OK.

Tomas   OK.

Ebba   OK.

Tomas   Yeah.

Ebba   Yeah.

Tomas   And he's done other stuff before this too that I hate.

Ebba   Like what?

Tomas   He lies. He's selfish. He avoids responsibility. He covers up mistakes, blames it on colleagues. He's just so detestable.

Beat.

He cheats at games. Even when he plays with the kids. There are no limits to his selfishness. You name it. He volunteers for work trips tells you he has no choice but he does it because he just wants a night away. He's jealous.

Ebba   What could you be possibly jealous of?

Tomas   Attention. Of how much attention you give the kids. He doesn't really know who his kids are. He's pathetic.

Beat.

So pathetic. I can't live with him any longer, I don't know how you've managed so long. But I can't live with him any longer and I don't want to. I don't want to live like this anymore! I'm sick of it!

Ebba   Tomas.

Tomas   I'm so ashamed. I don't deserve any of you. I don't. I don't deserve you and I don't deserve the kids.

Tomas *sobs real tears now.*

They're right not to trust me.

Beat.

I don't trust me either.

Ebba   Tomas.

Tomas   I hate myself.

Tomas *cries louder.*

This mountain!

Beat.

It was supposed to impress you.

Beat.

Ebba   Please, let's go inside.

Tomas   It's taken everything.

Tomas' *cries become hysterical.*

A neighbour opens a door to see what's going on? **Ebba** *smiles awkwardly.*

Several neighbours open their doors in various stages of undress to see what's going on.

The **Cleaner** *appears in the lift, surveys the scene, and presses the button to close the doors.*

Ebba   Come on. Please.

Tomas *is wailing.*

Another neighbour opens the door, **Ebba** *is humiliated.*

Ebba   Tomas! Now! Get up.

But **Tomas** *has slumped on the floor.*

Ebba   Tomas! Let's go inside. Tomas. Tomas! Tomas shut the fuck up now!

Ebba *tries another tack and soothes* **Tomas**.

Ebba   Come on . . .

Ebba *picks him up, but she can't open the door because she doesn't have a key, she must knock it.* **Tomas** *is weeping.* **Ebba** *is banging on the door.*

Ebba   Vera! Open the door! Vera! Open! VERA OPEN THE FUCKING DOOR.

Vera *opens the door.*

Harry   I said no shouting.

Ebba   I know, I know I'm sorry sweetie.

They walk into the hotel room.

Scene Twenty-Three

Hotel Room

Ebba *carries* **Tomas** *in*.

Vera   What's the matter with him?

Tomas *is wandering around and crying*.

Ebba   Tomas can you just sit down?

Tomas *slumps onto the floor pathetically*.

Harry   What happened?

Ebba   Tomas. You need to, pull yourself together. Look at me. Look at me.

Look at me. Breathe. Breathe. Tomas, please . . . Breathe. Tomas, you're upsetting the kids.

He can't stop crying.

Ebba   Tomas, please calm down.

Harry *approaches* **Tomas**.

Harry   Daddy? (*Worried*.) Daddy!

Ebba   Don't worry, Harry. Daddy's just a bit sad. He'll be fine.

Harry   Why? What's happened?

Ebba   Everything will be fine.

Vera   What's the matter, Daddy?! Have you told him you're divorcing him?

Ebba   What no?

Vera   What's happening? Daddy!/ Please! What's the matter Daddy?

Ebba   I haven't done anything!/ He's just sad. It'll pass.

Vera   Daddy please. It's OK. Daddy. We're here. We love you. It's OK. It's OK. Don't cry.

Vera *hugs* **Tomas** *and cries with him.* **Tomas** *can just about manage to put his arm around* **Vera**.

Harry   Daddy?

Harry *joins them and* **Tomas** *wraps his arms around his children.*

Harry   I love you Daddy. Don't cry. It's OK.

Vera   Daddy please . . .

The three of them cry together and **Ebba** *is traumatised by the pain her family is in.*

Vera   Mum! Come here. Mum, come here and hug Dad and show him you still love him. Come here, Mum. SHOW HIM!

Ebba *startles.*

Vera   Come here now and hug Dad.

But **Ebba** *can't do it – she's too shocked at what her family is going through.*

Vera   You have to do something!

Ebba   I know. I know.

Vera *goes back to hugging* **Tomas**.

Ebba *stands apart from them watching her worst nightmare and feeling responsible.*

Lights down.

Scene Twenty-Four

The Mountain

Ebba *leads the whole family in ski gear and they shuffle onto the mountain. No-one wants to be here except* **Ebba**. *The wind is strong and noisy, visibility is poor. They are surrounded by white.*

Ebba   Right it's our last day! Our last chance to ski the mountain let's make sure it's a good one. I think we can try a red run, and I think someone is ready for poles!

Harry   Oh yes finally!

Ebba   So come on let's get up there before it gets too cold.

Tomas   Visibility isn't great Ebba.

Vera   Yeah Mum is this safe?

Ebba   The run's marked out we just need to stick together.

Harry   We can't see anything.

Ebba   It'll be fine. Tomas you go first, Harry and Vera follow Dad and I'll come at the rear. It'll be fine, stay close where you see each other. If Dad stops I want you all to stop up mountain of Dad is that clear?

Harry   OK.

Vera   OK.

Ebba   Tomas?

Tomas   Fine.

The family set off reluctantly.

Ebba   Let's go.

They set off.

They ski down slowly.

Ebba   Everybody OK?

Harry   Yeah.

Vera Yeah!

Ebba Tomas?

Tomas OK. If you can't see, just follow the sounds.

They ski down it's really foggy.

Tomas *pulls up, followed by* **Vera** *and then* **Harry**.

Tomas Let's wait for Mum.

She doesn't appear.

Tomas Ebba? (*Shouting.*) Ebba? Ebba? Ebba? Ebba?

Nothing.

Vera Mum?

Tomas Ebba, can you hear me? Are you there?

A faint voice.

Tomas What?

Ebba (*in the distance*) Help!

Vera She said help! MUM!

Harry MUM!

Tomas OK OK. You wait here. Don't move. If you hear me calling your name call back so I can find you. Stay here. Stay together I'll go find her.

Vera Dad I'm scared.

Tomas It's fine, she'll be fine. I'll find her. Look after Harry.

Tomas *leaves.*

Tomas I'm coming, Ebba!

Tomas *runs back up the mountain.*

Tomas I'm coming don't move! I'm coming! Just keep calling out.

Ebba   Tomas!

Tomas *eventually finds* **Ebba** *sat in the snow, perfectly happy.*

Tomas   Are you OK?

Ebba   I'm fine.

Tomas   What happened?

Ebba   You need to save me.

Tomas   What's happened?

Ebba   Nothing, but the kids need to see you save me and then everything will be fine.

Tomas *hesitates.*

Ebba   What?

Tomas   But. I thought all of that . . . you know.

Ebba   I can't have another night like last night. So save me. And everything will get back to normal. Come on. Pick me up.

Tomas *is not sure what to do.*

Ebba   They're gonna be scared.

Tomas *jolts into action and carries* **Ebba** *down hill.*

Harry   He's been gone a long time.

Vera   Just wait.

They wait some more.

Harry   But how does he know where we are?

They wait some more.

Vera   Dad?

Harry   Daddy!

Vera   DAAAAAAD!/ DAAAAAAAD!

Harry   Daddy? Daddy . . . Daddy! Daddy? Daddy?

Tomas (*O/S*)   Harry!

Harry   Daddy!

Tomas (*O/S*)   Vera . . .

Tomas *emerges carrying* **Ebba** *down the mountain – the HERO.*

Vera   Mum! What happened?

Ebba   I think I twisted my knee. Your dad saved me.

Tomas   Everyone's safe now.

Harry   I was so scared we couldn't see you and we were shouting/ and it was just me and Vera and we couldn't see anything.

Ebba   Well lucky Dad could find me and carry me otherwise I don't know how long I would have been up there. Thank you Tomas.

Tomas   No problem.

Harry *hugs his dad.*

Tomas   Everyone's, everyone's safe now.

Vera *hugs* **Tomas**.

Ebba *smiles at* **Tomas** *but* **Tomas** *can't quite enjoy the moment.*

Ebba   Right I think Dad's right, it is a bit dangerous up here, let's go home and have some hot chocolates.

Vera   Yes!

Harry   Yes!

Ebba   I'm going in the front this time!

Ebba *skis off, followed by* **Harry** *and* **Vera**.

Tomas *looks up the mountain, he's got what he wants, but it feels hollow.*

He follows them off the mountain.

Lights down.

Scene Twenty-Five

Hotel Room

Tomas *lies on the sofa looking at his phone.*

Vera *is looking at her iPad.* **Harry** *is playing on his own and* **Ebba** *is packing the suitcases on her own. She looks at* **Tomas***.*

Ebba   Well this has been great. Hasn't it?

Mumbles of agreement.

Have you two thanked your father for the holiday? It's down to him we're able to afford things like this. Nice holidays.

Beat.

Because he works so hard. So can I hear some thank yous?

Vera   Thank you Dad.

Harry   Thanks Dad.

Ebba   Tomas?

Tomas   Hm?

Ebba   The kids are saying thank you for the holiday.

Tomas   You're welcome.

Ebba   Your daddy works very hard. We're very lucky. Aren't we? We are.

Tomas   OK.

Tomas *gets up but doesn't quite know where to go.*

Ebba   If anyone wants to lend a hand here I won't argue.

Nothing.

Anyone?

Beat.

Tomas?

Tomas   Hmm?

Ebba   Can you help please? We have a flight to catch.

Tomas *slowly heads over to the suitcases. He makes a half hearted attempt to help,* **Ebba** *watches him like a hawk. He has no idea what he should be doing. After a few beats he looks at his phone again.*

Ebba   Tomas.

Tomas *puts his phone away and tries packing again. It's slow and aimless.*

Ebba   Kids, time to pack.

Nothing from the kids.

Ebba   Right kids. Vera, stop that. Harry get your case. Let's everyone do their bit now, so we can check out on time. Come on. Vera. Harry. Teamwork. Work as a team.

Vera *doesn't flinch,* **Harry** *is wandering around.*

Ebba   I am not doing all this for you, you're old enough/ to pack your own things. Vera!

Harry   I'm looking for my sunglasses/ I want to wear them on the coach

Ebba   Vera.

Vera   In a minute.

Ebba   Not in a minute/ Vera, now.

Vera   I'm going to do it,/ I just haven't chosen what I'm wearing yet.

Ebba   Vera. VERA!

Vera   DON'T SHOUT AT ME.

Ebba   JUST PUT YOUR STUFF IN THE CASE.

Vera   I HAVEN'T CHOSEN WHAT TO WEAR YET.

Ebba   What you're wearing is fine pack your case and put it by the door!

Vera   YOU KNOW ONCE IT'S FULL I CAN'T LIFT IT.

Ebba   Well, Dad will lift the case for you, won't you Tomas?

Tomas   Of course.

Ebba   Get on with packing please.

Vera   Ok fine.

Ebba   Good girl.

Vera *starts packing*.

Ebba   And don't ever worry about lifting stuff Vera.

Beat.

We've got Dad. He's big and strong.

Tomas' *heart sinks,* **Ebba** *sees this*.

Ebba   What?

Tomas   Nothing.

Vera *is shoving things into the suitcase*.

Ebba   I'm just saying you'll do it. What?

Tomas   I don't/ know.

Harry   Has anyone seen my sunglasses?

Ebba   Harry/ just look! (*To* **Tomas**.) What?

Vera   There. Packed. Happy now? Ready for a big strong man!

Ebba   Don't speak/ to your father like that.

Tomas   They can see what you're doing . . .

Ebba   Apologise to your father.

Vera   What?

Ebba   Apologise. Now.

Vera   It was a joke. I was joking.

Ebba   Apologise.

Vera   I'm sorry.

Ebba   Normal voice.

Vera   I'm sorry.

Ebba   Now, give him a hug.

Vera   Seriously?

Tomas   Ebba.

Ebba   Hug your father.

Huffing, **Vera** *goes towards* **Tomas,** *but before she can get there.*

Tomas   Ughh actually my phone's ringing I've got to take it.

Tomas *pulls his phone out and heads for the door.*

Tomas   Hello?

Ebba *does not buy it . . . but* **Tomas** *is gone.*

Once he's out of the room **Tomas** *drops the deceit and is alone, but for once it's comforting.*

Scene Twenty-Six

The Lift

With their suitcases, the family head along the corridor.

Ebba   Can we take the stairs?

Tomas   With all this? Come on get in.

Tomas *presses the lift button.* **Ebba** *is anxious.*

Tomas *presses the lift doors again. The doors open and standing there are several other guests including* **Charlotte** *and* **Jenny** *and* **Mats** *with their luggage.*

Mats   Hey!

Jenny   Hey.

Tomas   Hi. Hi.

Charlotte   Hello.

Tomas   Come on. In you go. We can do it. Sorry. Sorry. In there. Put your hands down.

Tomas *ushers in the kids – it's a squeeze.*

Ebba *is reluctant.*

Ebba   I'll take the stairs it's too tight.

Vera   Mum, there's room.

Tomas   Yeah come on, it's fine.

Against her better judgement, **Ebba** *squeezes into the lift.*

The doors close.

Tomas   Ground floor please.

Mats   Alright.

Mats *presses the button.*

Nothing.

Mats *presses the button again.*

The lift starts to move.

MECHANICAL GROANS!

The lift judders!

Jenny   What was that?

MECHANICAL GROANS, AND THE SOUND OF METAL SHEARING, OR TEARING.

Ebba   What the hell was that?/ What was that noise? What was that?

Tomas   It's fine it's fine. It'll be something it's fine.

Everyone is looking up.

The lift jolts again and everyone screams!

Ebba   We have/ to get out we have to get out!

Jenny   Press the button/ Press the button!

Vera   Which/ one! I can't see it!

Mats   The/ alarm press the alarm.

Ebba   We have to get out/ we have to get out!

Charlotte   Whoa! Relax relax./ I'm sure it's fine.

Harry   I'm scared!

Tomas   It'll be OK/ it'll be OK.

Ebba   We have/ to get out now!

Tomas   Ebba, breath it's OK, we're OK . . .

Jenny   We have/ to ring someone now!

Tomas   Everyone calm/ down, calm down!

DEATHLY MECHANICAL SCREECHING!

Harry   Mum!

Vera   Mum what are you doing?

Ebba   LET ME OUT!/ I'VE GOT TO GET OUT I'VE GOT TO GET OUT!

Tomas   Eb/ ba!

Harry   MU/ MMY! MUMMY!

Vera   MUM!

Ebba *goes to the doors and with her bare hands, pulls the doors apart.*

Ebba *manages to prise the doors open just enough to climb out. She pulls herself up onto the floor of the Reception and runs away from the lift.*

Jenny   Get out before the doors close!

In the lift there is a surge of people trying to get out.

Mats   Whoa whoa whoa! Everyone back up. We're all getting out of here, but we're going to do it calmly and safely, women and children out first. Kids! Nice and calm.

Tomas *and* **Mats** *help the children out and then all the guests before climbing out of it themselves.*

Jenny   Are you OK?

Ebba *shakes her head.*

Ebba   We could have died! That thing's a death-trap. We need to sue them!

Jenny   You did the right thing. It was a good thing, getting out like that.

Ebba *runs to* **Harry** *and* **Vera** *and scoops them up.*

Vera   Are you OK?

Tomas   Everyone's fine.

Ebba   I'm so sorry, you know what I'm like in small spaces I just panicked but I want you to know you are the most precious things in Mummy's life and I love you so much, I just panicked, I'm so sorry. Can you forgive me?

Tomas *waits with bated breath.*

Harry   It's OK.

Vera   It's fine, we know/ you get claustrophobic.

Tomas *watches on – processing.*

Ebba   Oh thank you, you two are the most amazing kids any Mum could ever wish for I love you so much.

Ebba, **Harry** and **Vera** *hug each other tightly and* **Tomas** *stands outside of them, witnessing this honesty and vulnerability.*

Ebba *lets the kids go.*

Ebba (*to* **Tomas**)   I am so sorry.

Tomas   No I'm sorry.

Beat.

It's my fault I shouldn't have made you get in there. I know, how scary that must have been for you.

Ebba *hugs* **Tomas** *involuntarily.*

It takes them both by surprise, **Tomas** *returns the hug.*

It's the most affection they've shown each other all week. They needed it.

Tomas   We're all safe now.

Ebba *goes back to the kids.*

Ebba   It's all I could do, (*kissing the kids*) I'm sorry Mummy's so pathetic.

Vera   It's fine.

Harry   It's fine.

Mats   A manager's coming they asked us to wait everyone cool with that? Is that OK with everyone?

Everyone nods in understanding.

Tomas *looks at* **Ebba** *holding* **Harry** *and* **Vera** *tightly.*

Tomas   I'm gonna . . . step out . . .

Ebba *knows what this means, she nods approval.*

Scene Twenty-Seven

Outside the hotel

Tomas *steps out and stares at the mountain and he gets a cigarette out, but he's lost his light.*

He sees the **Cleaner** *smoking.*

Tomas   Avez-vous du feu? Ah thank you.

Beat.

Tomas *indicates the mountain.*

Skiez-vous?

Cleaner (*gets up and leaves*)   Non. Je bois trop.

Tomas   Ah . . .

Tomas *turns and sees* **Harry** *staring at him.*

Harry   Do you smoke?

Tomas   No. no . . .

Tomas *tries hiding the cigarette.*

Harry   What's that then?

Beat.

Tomas   It's . . . um . . . ugh . . . well . . .

Tomas *sees his son – he's not an idiot.*

Actually, Harry, ask me again.

Harry   Do you smoke?

Tomas   Yes.

Beat.

I'm trying to quit. And I'm. I'm finding it, hard. Really hard at the moment. But. You know. I'm gonna really try to stop when we get back home. Is that OK?

Harry   I don't want you to die.

Tomas   I know. I know. Me too I don't want to die either.

Beat.

I'm sorry.

Beat.

It's a stupid habit and I'm . . . I hide it from you because, well because I'm ashamed. When we get home I'm going to really try hard to quit.

Harry   OK.

Tomas   OK. Come here.

Harry *gives him a hug and then he runs around in the snow.*

Tomas *looks at his cigarette – might as well finish it. He enjoys smoking and watching* **Harry** *playing.*

Vera *and* **Ebba** *come out.*

Harry   Dad smokes.

Vera   I know.

Tomas   W/ hat?

Harry   He's going to quit when we get home.

Tomas   You knew? For how long.

Vera *shrugs.*

Tomas   Well . . . when we get back . . . I'm going to quit I promise. Vera.

Vera   OK.

Tomas   I promise.

Vera   OK.

Vera *joins* **Harry** *playing with the snow.*

Tomas *looks to* **Ebba,** *a new way of being with the family has been found.*

Tomas *turns to the mountain and blows smoke towards it.*

The End.